The JFDI Way To Increasing Profits Through Outstanding Customer Service

This is a work of non-fiction. This publication is designed to provide accurate information on the subject matter covered. It is sold on the understanding that the publisher is not engaged in rendering professional services or advice. The information is not intended to replace any legal council or other professional directives. If the professional services or advice or other assistance is required, the services of a professional should be sought.

ISBN 978-0-615-63939-0

Library of Congress Control: On File With The Publisher

Published by JFDI Publishings
       www.JFDIPublishings.com

This Book may be ordered by visiting www.JFDIPublishings.com

Printed In The United States of America

Business/Customer Service

The JFDI Way To Increasing Profits Through Outstanding Customer Service

By

Ian Houghton

Foreword By

Nik Halik

Acknowledgments

I could not have completed this book without the love and support of my family and friends. These people are the ones who have continually pushed and inspired me to make my life what it is, and what it is becoming. I am deeply grateful for all you have done for me and continue to do for me.

First of all I would like to thank my mother and father, Linda and Ken Houghton, who have always supported and loved me unconditionally, even when I was a nightmare as a child. Without you both I would not be the person I am today, you have always inspired me and pushed me to become better and better and for that I thank you. My brother and sister in-law, David and Claudette, both of you have always been there for me when I needed love and support, you never questioned anything but loved me and were there for me no matter what was going on in my life. My two nephews, Josh and Jake. Boys... if Uncle Ian can do this you can too! Life is an amazing gift, live a life of passion, dream big and 'make it happen'. Do what you always want to do in life and what puts a smile on your face every single day. You will be repaid in ways you never knew possible.

To my Nanna and Grandpa, Dorothy and Arthur Paxton two of the most incredible human beings on the planet. You always went above and beyond as grandparents helping guide me through my life and giving me total unconditional love and support at all times, without you both I would not be the person I am today. To my Auntie and Uncle, Andrea and Mike Macara, two of the most loving and caring people you could wish to meet, you would and have done anything for me and for that I thank you. To my cousins, Nick and Amy, guys, give life a real go, don't mess around. Figure out what your dream is and pursue it with unquestioning passion, trust and faith and JFDI!

To my friends......Nik Halik meeting you changed my life. You have inspired me more than you can possibly imagine, not only are you unbelievably inspirational but you are one of the nicest people I have ever known. It's a total privilege to call you a best friend, when we get together all we do is laugh, laugh, laugh, like two naughty school kids, my life is what it is today because of you... and..... delete! :0) To Marie-Helene Legare, you are an amazingly intelligent woman, there is no question that this book would not be what it is without all the hard work, effort and support you have given me. You had such faith in me and constantly kept pushing me to provide the best information possible in helping to teach others, and for that I thank you. I am very grateful to have you in my life. To Jodi Nicholson, without you this book would never have come about, you focused me on what I needed to do, you planted seeds that started to grow, so thank you. I would also like to thank Barry and Deb Schlouch who reminded me that everything we ever need in life is love, to both give and receive. I now understand that it's those individuals who are most passionate about what they do that truly succeed in life, so, thank you!

To all my clients and customers past, present and future. You are the whole reason I do what I do, you recognize my passion and allow me to help you to become better, thank you.

Last but not least to Tony Robbins, Robert Kiyosaki and Frank Kern, these three people have changed my life more than I could have possibly imagined. Your teachings made me have a complete mind shift and forced me to start thinking differently. I always believed that we should lead from the heart and with your teachings you reinforced what I had always believed to be true.

Foreword

You Are Mere Moments From Discovering How Others JUST LIKE YOU, Have Seen Their Business Explode In Significant Profits From Simply Reading this Informative And In Depth Manifesto About The Greatest Keys To Business Success.

Never have I read such a deep reaching book which dissects the entire process of value-facturing your clients needs than The JFDI Way To Increasing Profits Through 'Outstanding' Customer Service by Ian Houghton. Prepare to witness an epic revolution of exponential business growth. There is only one valid definition of business purpose: to create a customer. It is the customer who determines what a business is.

Customers are continuously adapting to their ever-changing environments. They're now more educated, better informed, more value conscious and demand more for their dollar. They're no longer willing to be pushed around anymore by businesses. In short, they want better customer service. As Ian Houghton will tell you, this can literally make or break you.

You're in business to generate profits by selling your products and services to people who need and want to buy. Customers want to know how you can transform their lives and quite possibly relieving them of their pain. Great marketing acquires new customers for you, but it's great customer service that ensures that the customers keep coming back to you. Your most pivotal and optimized marketing push is to incorporate everything you are about to read in The JFDI Way To Increasing Profits Through 'Outstanding' Customer Service.

Good customer service is all about bringing customers back. It's about sending them away happy - happy enough to pass on positive feedback about your business along to others. How do you go about forming such a relationship? By remembering the one true secret of good customer service and acting accordingly; As Ian will tell you in The JFDI Way To Increasing Profits Through 'Outstanding' Customer Service. "You will be judged by what you do, not what you say."

Good customer service is the lifeblood of any business. The lifeblood of your business will only be validated if you apply every principle and technique you adapt from this fascinating read.

Nik Halik

International Speaker, Best Selling Author,
Global Investor, Astronaut and Adventurer

TABLE OF CONTENTS

Introduction

First of all let me congratulate you on choosing this book. The simple fact that you've chosen to seek advice on Customer Service means you are way ahead of the game, and at the very least you are curious to learn how customer service can have a positive effect on your business profits.

What is the JFDI way? Well it's what I say when someone just needs to do something. People often talk about doing this or doing that, but never actually really end up doing anything, they never action anything. *Success is ALL about action, knowledge is just knowledge, action is power,* so 'Just F****** do it'! Stop messing around, stop wasting time, and put it into action, 'Just F****** do it'!

So, what is the point of this book? Well, it's very simple. It's to raise your awareness level about where people so often get it *wrong* in business: customer service. Then, once you *do* become aware of the importance of customer service and some of the so often overlooked pitfalls, taking action will have significant positive impacts for your business.

So many people look for so many different areas in their business to increase profits. Yet, what so many of them fail to realize is that they don't look after their customers well enough... If you don't look after them properly, where will they go...? Simple, they're going to find someone that offers what you offer, but someone who does it *better*.

The whole point of this book is to help you understand what the customer needs and then to make the changes within your own business to meet those needs. One of the absolute best ways to do this is to look for some of the real quality businesses within your industry, and see how they do it. What makes them different? How do they go about their business practices that are different from yours?

I have a huge passion for business. I have a huge passion for my customers and for customers in general. Why is that? Because, I believe this: if a customer is handing over their hard-earned money to you, then in return they deserve to have us look after them. But, what you find nowadays is that so many businesses really seem to have forgotten all about this, and all they seem interested in is just the initial sale.

Well, the initial sale is great. It brings in money upfront, but, if you're not looking after that customer in the long-term, then they're going to go elsewhere. It's pretty obvious wouldn't you agree? I'm sure you've come across this yourself when you've been to a restaurant, for example.

If the restaurant's food is excellent and the restaurant is beautiful, that's great. Yet, if you go there and you dine on great food, but the service is awful, then you're unlikely to go back. I know that sometimes this is a tough decision, especially when the restaurant is exceptional with its food or is an exceptional-looking restaurant. Sometimes we fight this battle in our heads: "Well, I don't really want to go back there because I don't really enjoy being treated that way. Yet, I want to go back because I really like the food and I love the place." So it puts you in a dilemma, do I go back or don't I?

Now, imagine if you feel that, do you think that you're the *only* customer feeling that way? Absolutely not. So, it's important to understand that by looking at a customer almost as if they are a friend, and taking care of them properly, this friend - this customer - will come back and look after *you* in return. They'll look after you by remaining loyal by continuing to buy your products and services – bringing you their hard earned money. That's why we are in business, to make money to pay off expenses and to make enough profit so we can pull a decent income. But, like I said, so many business owners see a customer walk through their door or go to visit a customer, and they look at the customer with pound or dollar signs flashing in their eyes, and they pay very little attention to what the customer's actual needs are.

So, the point of this book is to increase your consciousness when it comes to customer service within your business. You may feel that you look after your customers exceptionally well. Well, I believe I do too, but there is always room for improvement. There are always new and different ways that you can look after the customers, and it's up to you to find out what those ways are. We're going to cover a bunch of different ways in this book. Understand that the education process doesn't just finish the moment you read the last page in this book. In fact, if anything, the education has only just started, because hopefully this is going to get you into such a mindset that you're going to want to seek out more information. So, be aware as to what is out there right now, and take time to assess how you look after your customers; make some notes.

Let's say you own a business with a customer base already attached to it. Pull yourself away from the fact that you're the owner of that business. Now, if you are a consultant or even a friend going into that business, how would you look after a customer better? If you were the customer dealing with that business, how would you want to be looked after?

These are the things that you now need to start looking at, and by making small tweaks within your business here and there you're going to find that customers are going to want to stay with you.

As a child, I grew up with a business background. My great-grandfather started a business in 1953, and it's still held by our family today. The family was fairly successful. They did what they knew was right to do, and that was to look after their customers. As a child growing up, I remember thinking: "Well, sure that's common sense that we look after the customers. We treat them with respect; we treat them with care, and if our product or service isn't right for them, then it's our duty and responsibility to let them know it's okay if they don't buy from us." The reason? Because then we start to work off of our referrals, don't we? That customer passes on the word about how good we are. Even if our product or service isn't right for them at that *point*, they might know someone for whom it *is* right. In addition, maybe in the future our product will be what they need, and they'll remember that we put *their* needs ahead of *our* profit.

Yet, I often find that so many businesses are not the slightest bit bothered about the customer. Often they even get upset if the customer doesn't buy from them there and then, they think the customer has just wasted their time. What they really fail to realize is that they're building up their customer base. These customers are free advertising for them, and sometimes we need to just look at things in a slightly different way.

Free advertising. How on earth could a customer be free advertising?

They might not buy your product or service, but they may send someone that does. They may send a *hundred* people, but you just don't know that. Word of mouth advertising is one of the most powerful there is. Look at movies; how many have had multi-million dollar advertising budgets, and been flops? Yet, on the flipside, think of the modest films that have been huge hits, despite virtually zero advertising. How were they hits? Word of mouth! So that is why it's so important to look after customers. Growing up I remember looking at all these businesses thinking: "You just don't really genuinely seem to care. You're doing this purely to watch that money come in".

Well, when you come from a place of money, money, money, even though the universe may bring you that money, it's not going to bring you what you really deserve when you really focus on looking after the customer. Because, when you focus on the customer and how you can benefit them in your business, then you, personally come from a different place internally and the customer recognizes this. You're not coming from the place of money anymore; you're coming from a place of being able to add value to their life. You are a value-facture; you manufacture value.

How can you increase the value every time you are in front of a customer? It might be one person or it might be a hundred people all in one go. How can you find new ways that are outside of the norm?

You see, every industry has a norm. This is how they "do it" in that industry; how they conduct business. That doesn't always mean it's the right way to do it and, in fact, usually when you follow what goes on within your industry, you start to limit yourself and your business. You start to look at your company and say: "Well, actually, I don't need to do any more than this because this is just what my industry is doing anyway." But, the whole point of a successful business is to go above and beyond.

16

It is to give the customer an experience so that when they deal with you, they walk away and say: "I can't believe that just happened to me, it was amazing. In fact, I've got to tell my friends." Or, nowadays this happens: "I'm going to put on Facebook what just happened," or "I'm going to Tweet what's happening". At the same time, let's look at that from the negative perspective. What happens if they receive bad service? Well, they can do the same thing. They can tell their friends, they can tell their family. They can Facebook it and they can Tweet it. They can get that message around. With the Internet being the way it is nowadays, we are all open to being reviewed.

If you go onto Amazon and you buy a book or a digital camera or something else, if you're anything like me, you'll read some of the reviews. What are *real* people saying about the product? When the Internet first came out, we used to have sales page websites, and this was our opportunity to get across who we were and what we did in order for the customer to come to us so we could make the sale. But, nowadays the way people are able to post reviews, now more than ever it is so important to be aware what bad reviews can do to you and your business.

So, it is important, therefore, to look at the way your business currently runs and say: "How can I make the service better for the customer?" "How can I *now* give outstanding service?" As I said, there are a number of different ways we can do this, and that's what we're going to cover in this book. If you want to get started on this immediately, ask some family and friends. Say to them: "Have you ever noticed anything about my business? Have you noticed anything that I do that is really good or really bad?" Because what you want to do is weed out the bad stuff and start to increase the good in your business.

So many people are unaware of the things they do on a daily basis both in their personal and business lives, so that when good things happen they don't know how they happened. I use a great analogy of two golfers. I was brought up in a family background that just happened to like golf. So, growing up in the UK, my father always used to watch Nick Faldo, who is a very systematic golfer. He knew what he did every single time he addressed the ball, and then there was another golfer, Seve Ballesteros, who was a naturally gifted golfer. The problem was this: when someone is naturally gifted at something, they don't know how to fix it when it goes wrong...

When Seve Ballesteros had a bad game, he didn't know how to pull his game back. He didn't know because he didn't know where he was going wrong. On the other hand, Nick Faldo knew what he was doing wrong. He would approach the ball, and go through a number of steps in his mind. "I have to do this, I have to do that, I have to do this. I have to do this." Very systematic, but the benefit for him was that he knew the moment his game was off, he could just address the ball again and go through his systematic steps and pull his game back.

By becoming consciously aware of what works and what doesn't work, both in business and in our personal life, this is when we can consciously start to make the changes necessary to improve both areas of our life.

So, consciously become aware of what works well in your business, what works well in customer service. The next time you get good feedback from a customer, analyze what you did in order to get that good feedback. Then make sure you do it over and over and over again. Make it part of regularly doing business with you; because the moment you do that, not only do you massively increase customer service, but you *start to improve the overall experience of doing business with you.* When you create a positive customer experience every single time, that customer will come back over and over and over again. This is where it becomes powerful!

I know you have experienced this in something you can relate to right now. Think of a business or even an individual that you like being around and now think about what it is that you like about them, and I virtually guarantee that they add value to your life. They enhance your life. They make your life better. That is why you keep going back to them. So, if you look after your customers the way your friends and businesses look after you, and you offer an experience like that to your customers, they will absolutely keep coming back.

Take some time now and think to yourself: "Okay, what do I do that I *know* gets an outstanding reaction from my customers?" What is that? Make some notes now. Get a notebook or go to the notes page at the end of each chapter right now and start making notes. By the end of reading the book, you'll be able to look at it and say: "Oh, I can start to implement this, I can do that, I can do this, I can do that."

The intention of this is that you walk away at the end of this book, or each chapter, with ideas to help you increase the level of your service, and therefore start to begin to build raving fans that want to come back to you over and over again. They want to come back to you because you are genuine, you are sincere, and you are the *best* at what you do.

www.ianhoughton.com

<u>Notes:</u>

How would you want to be looked after as a customer?

What do you do that you *know* gets an outstanding reaction from your customers?

What do you do better than others when it comes to customer service?

How can you find ways that are outside of the norm yet can be applied within your industry?

How can you increase the value every time you are in front of a customer?

Introduction

Chapter 1: Why Outstanding Customer Service is So Important

As a child, I noticed that customers used to love dealing with my family, and I could never really understand why that was. Obviously, I get it now, but as a child I wondered: "Why are these customers really loving my family right now?" It finally dawned on me that it was because my family genuinely cared. They cared about what they did and they cared about their customers. They weren't just interested in making the money. I mean, obviously they were interested in making money; they wouldn't be in business if they weren't, but it wasn't *just* about the money for them. It was about the fact that they were able to touch somebody else's life. When a customer bought a product from them they were overjoyed. They received a great comment about their business, they saw a smile on the customer's face and they knew that all of their hard work was worthwhile.

I've noticed over my years of growing up, and certainly moving from the UK to the US, how the service standard has slipped; not just a little bit either, but massively slipped.

I remember being a kid, and I was really lucky: My parents loved to travel, so they would always have one holiday for themselves each year and then we would have a family holiday. I remember coming to America when I was a little boy. In fact, we came to the same part of America that I now live in. We always used to go to Disney World, and it was one of those places that is really magical. But that magic went beyond seeing Mickey Mouse and all those famous and loving characters walking around. It was the way that everybody was just so friendly. They were so happy. Not only were they happy, but the property was immaculate. The grounds were incredible. The staff always went above and beyond. They didn't just do enough to make the sale.

Walt Disney could have said: "I'll tell you what we'll do. We'll build this up, we'll make it look really, really good and then the moment we get somebody coming through the door that buys a ticket we'll just forget about them." But no, his attitude was about experiencing magic. The moment somebody walks through the door, that is when they get the *experience*. They get to see how much Disney cared by giving them the most incredible service they've ever experienced. That is why Disney is as strong as it is today. They really sell an experience, don't they? When you come away from Disney World what memories do you have? If you have not been to Disney, go there. Experience it.

The truth of the matter is, if you've been to Disney World once, you've probably been there twice. Maybe you've been there three or four times, or more. The reason *you go back is because of the service and experience you get.* Otherwise, there are a bunch of other theme parks that you can go to, aren't there? But Disney World is special. They treat you like when you were kids and they allow you to have fun, and they look after you and take care of you. They show this by the service they provide and they also back it up with a phenomenal experience.

You walk out with empty wallets, and you don't care, because you just had a great day and an outstanding experience, and you'll go back and empty your wallet again, that's the level of service and experience I'm talking about.

When I moved to America, I noticed how service had really slipped, whereas service levels were on the increase in the UK. My family always used to make notes of things that they would see on their travels and then they would implement them within their business, they would JFDI, these were things to increase the level of service for their customer. The reason people continue to go back to Disney over and over again is because Disney is fully aware about the importance of creating raving fans in their customers. They are fully aware about the lifetime value of a customer. Yet when we go to other people's businesses now, we see how they're just interested in that initial sale. They don't care about anything more than taking your money from you.

If Disney had done that back in the day, would the company still be around today? Maybe, maybe not, but if they had done that and stuck to it, they surely wouldn't be the company they've always been. The whole point of this is that when we start to produce raving fans as customers, then our job becomes easier because they want to help you in return. I know you've experienced this before in your own life: you have such a great experience in dealing with an individual or a business that you want to send them customers. So it's really important to look at the service in your business and say: "How can I make this better? What do I need to do? Where am I letting myself and my customers down?"

I'll tell you how you can find out how you're letting yourself down. Look at where the majority of your complaints come from. What area of your business is it? Do you have a customer service philosophy? It has become more evident to me as time goes by how little businesses really focus on their customers. *Really* focus on giving them 'outstanding' service, *giving them an experience every single time they do business with you.* I see it all the time with the businesses I deal with. You walk in, the service is just enough to get the sale. The staff are just good enough to do their job. They're just motivated enough to climb out of bed and put their clothes on.

So, it's time to start becoming aware of all these things around you. Like I said in the previous chapter, when something good happens in your business that should be a trigger. A light bulb should go on in your head. You should have your "aha" moment. "What just happened? What did I do to get that outstanding response?" Then make a note of it, and figure out what you can give back to your customers all the time to every customer, and the same on the bad side. When something bad happens, there should be a light bulb going on, an "aha" moment again, an: "Oh, right, I get it. I just made a mistake". Again, what did you do, what did you say, or what didn't you do or say? Make a note of it. Make sure it doesn't happen again.

Obviously, this is so crucially important in your business because you want that customer to keep coming back. You want to give them a level of service that makes them say: "WOW", because when they receive that "WOW" service, when they receive that "thing" you've just done for them, they'll want to continue coming back. Why is that important? Because you want your customers to come back to you over and over again.

www.ianhoughton.com

We spend so much time in business constantly trying to find new customers. One of my favorite analogies to best explain this is to think of a bucket of water. Imagine it being your business, filled with customers. But the bottom of the bucket is full of little holes. Each one of those holes is an issue your customers have with your business. So, what happens to the water? It just falls out the bottom. You pour more in to fill it again, and the water goes. The same with your customers. What happens when your customers fall out of your business? What do you do? You generally spend vast amounts of money on things like advertising and mail shots to find new customers so you can put them in the bucket, and then what happens? They fall out the bottom too. Some will buy, some won't. What happens then? You go and spend even more money to get still more customers. You stick them in the bucket. So, now they fall out the bottom too. Are we starting to notice a pattern here? If we always do what we've always done – we will always get what we've always got. What do we want to do? How about we take some of that money we spend on advertising and mail shots and spend it fixing some of those holes in the bucket, by looking after our existing customers.

So, let's imagine that we've taken this bucket and we've filled in the little holes. Now we pour the water in. What happens? Where does the water go? Where do the customers go? They stay there because you've looked after them; because you've taken care of them. You've done more than what anybody else in your industry does. This is why it's so important. Everybody is always looking to try and find new customers. **Yet, we fail to realize that the *existing* customers we have are really where our true success and true wealth lies.** It's not about going out and finding new customers all the time. It's about looking after and working on existing customers because your existing customers will help bring in new customers. You have to do what you can to keep them. You look after them,

28

care about them. Communicate with them like they're your best friend. Have constant communication with them, but don't try to sell to them all the time because people are not stupid. I am not stupid. Are you? I'm sure you're not. It's about looking after them. It's about being genuine. It's about being sincere, and when the customer sees that, they don't *want* to go anywhere else. Why should they? They want to stay with you. You care about them. They now care about you. It's as simple as that. Guess what – soon you are going to need a bigger bucket!

<u>Notes:</u>

Do you have a customer service philosophy, if so what is it?

What do you do that gets an outstanding and negative response from your customers?

What areas of your business do you get the majority of your complaints from?

Where are you letting yourself and your customers down? How can you make your service better?

What do you need to do to improve your service?

Chapter 2: How My Family Business Knew About This and How It Changed My Life Growing Up

I mentioned before, I was really lucky that my parents used to love to travel. As I said, we came to America a great deal, and we learned so much back then. America had really grasped an understanding of customer service and they were really, really good at it, and the really good businesses would even throw an experience in that would make you say "WOW". Some businesses still are really good at it. I think we also probably know that a bunch of the businesses in America and the UK have lost it. They've lost their way, they've lost their path, and they've lost their focus. They're confused, and they're out there looking for something to help them.

Now, I see it from a British perspective. I remember coming here, and America was *the* place, you used to be looked after so amazingly. We used to go to the restaurants and the service was phenomenal. You could go anywhere, you could go into a store, a shop to buy anything: clothes, a car, a house, you name it; you could buy a piece of chocolate, and the service was exceptional. Over time, I believe that businesses started to get arrogant and cocky. They became flippant with the customer. They didn't really care about them, and why should they? They were making a ton of money, but as easy as the money comes, it's just as easy for it to go. The point of this is that we want to make sure that money keeps coming in so we have a more profitable business, so we can become more successful as individuals. Become more successful *now* by looking after the customer, by taking care of them, by going above and beyond, and you'll be successful in the future.

I remember when we came to America as kids; how my mother and father would see something they just loved. If it was an outstanding example of customer service, they would be there taking photos of it, and they would make notes. I remember, I was probably about eleven or twelve years old, my parents took me to Thailand, and it was the first time we ever travelled to anywhere with such a big cultural difference. We saw service on a level that none of us had ever experienced before. We knew good service, but service in Thailand was on a whole new level. When they looked after us they did it from their heart. They genuinely cared about us. They wanted more than anything else to see us happy.

The staff that worked there didn't have the greatest of lives. They didn't come from wealth, and the majority of these people were living with their families, and when I say families, I'm talking extended families -- spouse, children, parents, grandparents, brothers, sisters and their children. Yet, when they walked into work every day to take care of us as customers, we knew nothing. We knew nothing except the fact that we saw this beaming smile on their face. They always went above and beyond. If something wasn't available for us, they'd go make it happen. They'd figured it out. They did what it took to make it happen. Just incredible service; I mean, incredible service.

Here I am now a number of years older and I still see it and feel it and experience it. Just writing about it now, I'm reliving the memory. Do you know what was so crazy about all of that? Do you know how much it cost them to do this? Nothing. Service is free, isn't it? Being a nice, genuine and caring person, and caring about others is free. Being attentive to their customers needs, going above and beyond. Putting a smile on their face. Caring about their customers. Making sure they are okay. It's free. It's all free. It always has been and it always will be.

Do you want to know one of the BIG secrets to giving outstanding service? Employ nice people, people who enjoy making others happy and who take pride in what they do. Take a look at your current staff. Are they the right ones to take your business to where you want it to be? If not, make the changes you need to make right now, this instant. If you don't, your business might not be around for long. Did you know that only 4% of businesses will make it to 10 years in business. Scary thought isn't it!

So, I saw that my parents would constantly make notes of all of the things they saw. Like I said, they'd take photos and then they'd take them back, and they would immediately implement what they had seen within their business, they would JFDI. Immediately. The speed of implementation. How fast from when you see something you like does it take for it to actually happen within a business?

A lot of people procrastinate. A lot of people put off: "I'm going to get around to this and that," or "I'll do this whenever I can." There's always something that gets in the way of our actions. **The only thing that *really* stops us from doing what we want to do in life is the story we have for why we can't do it.** "Oh, I can't implement this new customer service system right now because I have this going on," or "I can't do it because of whatever-it-may-be." Stop the excuses and JFDI!

Change the story, change the outcome; highly successful businesses begin things quickly. Now, sometimes they may not even be right. They may do something, and it might turn out to be a mistake, but you know what? Think about this: the moment you start something, you've started a process. You've started that ball rolling. Now, the hardest part to get that ball rolling was the initial push, wasn't it? That was the most difficult part. But now the ball is rolling, we can change its direction, if we want. The company starts to look at it and say: "Well, okay that actually is not the path I intend for this to go down. We can now change the direction we want this to go."

The truth of the matter is that all top successful businesses make a decision and they put it into action quickly, they JFDI. Then they notice the customer's reactions. Does the customer like it? Does the customer not like it?

I remember seeing my parents do this all the time. They'd be traveling around, and they'd say: "I love the idea of that. I'm taking that and implementing it in my business." They'd take it and implement it, and then watch the customer's reaction. Did it go over well or did it not go over well?

www.ianhoughton.com

I remember traveling to Hong Kong straight after our trip to Thailand. I was actually really upset about it. I remember it very, very vividly because I went from being treated so well as a tourist and customer in Thailand, with people that genuinely cared about me, to being in a huge city, Hong Kong, where the attention to details simply wasn't there. It didn't feel the same.

I remember as a kid actually being incredibly depressed by this. First two or three weeks after returning, it really hurt me; it really hurt my feelings. I remember getting back to the UK and saying to myself: "Why did I go? Why did they take me to Hong Kong? It ruined my holiday." It didn't, looking back on it *now*. In fact, what it *did* do was give me the knowledge that I am now able to pass on to you.

The reason Thailand was so exceptional was because of the experience I had there, and that experience was through *service*. I wasn't doing anything extraordinary. There wasn't an activity that I did that was incredible. It all had to do with the people. It all had to do with the service. It all had to do with the way they made me feel. It was all about the way they went above and beyond, not now and then but every single time.

It was the little things. They'd remember your name. These were the members of staff in big hotels; big hotels that had new customers coming in every single day. Yet, they knew your name. It was like: "Wow, they actually remember my name." It had been maybe a day or two since I'd been in the hotel. I'd been out here and there; I'd been out with my parents going to look at this, going to see that, and yet, when I came back, they still remembered my name. Not only did they remember my name, they knew that I liked a glass of Coke; so I'd walk into the hotel and a glass of Coke would be waiting for me. Not only would the Coke be waiting for me, but they knew that I didn't like ice in my Coke back then. Don't ask why; I couldn't tell you. I didn't like ice in my Coke, and that was that. So, I'd walk through the door of the hotel and they'd be standing there with a tray, a glass of Coke and no ice, and whatever my brother, mother and father wanted because they knew that was what we liked to drink, they cared. They seemed so happy to see us happy.

36

They would stand there with the biggest smiles on their faces like the whole reason they were put on this planet was to take care of us, to look after us, and I'd never experienced anything like that before in my life. To this day it still holds a real special place in my heart, and every single thing I have just said was free. It was all free.

They didn't do it because they were told to do it. They did it because they came from a place internally of love, of care, of looking after other people. They were the nicest most genuine people you'll possibly ever come across. I know it's not just that nation. We can find such genuine and caring individuals in nations all over the world, including the UK and America.

But as time has gone by, I think some of us may have lost what's important. We've focused on the money. I notice it so much. I moved to America about 18 months before the financial crisis hit. It was about the middle of 2005. I came from a place that is very real estate oriented. People in the UK very rarely invest in stocks and shares. They know nothing about them, but what they do know and understand is property. So, I've always seen in my life in the UK the property market going up and then going bust, and then going up and then going bust again. So, when I moved to America, I saw that property was absolutely absurdly crazy, prices were getting out of control, and loans were just being fabricated out of thin air. Lenders were lending anyone money. This had disaster written all over it. But, people didn't care back then. They didn't care how they ran their business because business was easy back then. So, they didn't have to look after the customer. We sit in an economy right now where, if you don't look after the customer, you are in big trouble, because someone else will happily look after your customer and steal them from you. Yet, I would say a huge percentage of businesses still haven't made the necessary changes and continue to operate like the economy is great. Even when the economy was great, they had real negative aspects to their business methods, and that was when they stopped caring. It was about the money, it wasn't about the customer.

So, as time went by through my years of growing up, it became more and more evident to me how passionate I was about getting my message out there. About getting out what I'd learned and seen, and the input within my own businesses that made me successful. It wasn't until only a couple of years ago that I realized: "Hang on a minute. Every single thing that I am doing here, everything that I've done that has been successful in my life has been because I've given outstanding customer service". I've always gone above and beyond, and in some businesses that failed, I took my eyes off the ball and I stopped focusing on the customer. Business was good, money was easy, it came in easy. I didn't have to care; so when I talk about this stuff, I don't talk about it flippantly like I don't know what I'm talking about. I've been there. I know what it's like to forget how important the customer is. Got the book, got the t-shirt and the movie!

How about we change the phrase "Customer Service" and replace it with "the Source-of-our-Profit Service". Would that help change how you viewed things?

A couple of years ago I decided I had to get this message of mine out there. I had to tell people it's time to start getting back to old-fashioned business values: looking after our customers is the source of our profit.

No doubt you can tell that going to all those countries when I was growing up had a massive positive impact in my life. And yet, all of it was so stupidly simple. Most of us simply miss the mark. We miss the mark because we lose our focus in business. Things get tough. Things get hard. I know what it's like. I've been there. I've made a bunch of money; I've lost a bunch of money. I've had great times; I've had really really tough times. I've had times that are so tough, so painful, that I'll never want to go through them again, and that's because I lost my focus. So, the point of this is to refocus you on what is important. What is important and what will always be important is the customer.

Notes:

Take a look at your current staff. Are they the right ones to take your business to where you want it to be?

Do your staff need training?

Notice the customer's reactions to the things you do or your staff does. What generates a positive reaction? What generates a negative reaction?

Chapter 3: How So Many Businesses Don't Look After The Customer

I know it is not just me who's experienced this, but I come into contact with so many businesses on personal and business levels, and the experience of doing business with them is sometimes absolutely shocking.

I could give you many examples of how many businesses get it wrong and where they get it wrong. You want to see an example of bad customer service? Go and visit two, three, four places of business today. Pick up the phone, call some people in business, and see how you get treated. You'll be absolutely 'gob-smacked' – a British word for amazed, jaw-dropping. You'll be 'gob-smacked' how, the more businesses you come into contact with, you can see the level of service they have, and be amazed at how bad their service is.

But, the thing is this: although it's bad, it's great for you because what you're doing now is recognizing the areas where so many people fail in their business. So, how can we make it better? Well, we just do the opposite of what they do. When they mess it up, we become consciously aware of it, and we make a positive change in our business.

Air Travel is only as safe as it is today because after each accident, exhaustive research and examination was done to find out what went wrong, and how they could ensure that the same accident couldn't happen again. So take that concept and introduce it into your business TODAY – JFDI!!!!

So now, when someone in our industry treats their customer bad, we are ready to step in and take the customer away from them, and amaze them with the way we will always go above and beyond in our business. We now want to give them outstanding levels of service.

It's not about just doing enough to look after them. It's about really caring. Spend some time right now and think about businesses you've recently visited and which ones offered you good service, and which offered you bad. What did they do that was bad? What was it? Make a note of it right now. Was it one business? Was it two businesses? Was it fifty? What were those things they did? Is there a pattern there? Are a lot of people making the same common mistakes? If so, what are they? Be aware of what they are because once you are, you can fix them, right?

Again, I mentioned in the previous chapter that I believe that the majority of these businesses don't have outstanding customer service. They may just not even be aware of service. It may be the fact that business is just too easy for them right now and they don't need to worry about it.

Now, look at the businesses that have outstanding service. What did they do? How did they treat you? What was it that made them different? If you just called the business on the telephone and they had outstanding service, why was it outstanding? Was it the individual you spoke to? If it was, what was it about that person? Become aware now of what it was that that individual did that was exceptional.

Make a note of all things you see and hear. Make a list of all the things you can think of, that you've experienced, that you think are awesome. Then, in a later chapter, we're going to look at how we can start putting some of these items within our business to increase our service.

So, we know that a huge percentage of businesses put very little effort, or no relevance, in looking after the customer. If this was an area you've focused on, even if it was for a short period of time, and when I say short, let's say a couple of months, you're going to start to set yourself above other businesses because they know that when they deal with you that they'll be receiving outstanding service. This is what is going to make your customers stay with you all the time. They'll want to keep coming back to you because you look after them better than anybody else, because you take care of them better than anybody else. This is what it's all about. It's about you separating yourself from everybody else by going above and beyond for the customer, by becoming consciously aware of both good and bad in your business and in other businesses. It's about leading from the heart and not the pocket. **It's about being Outstanding!**

www.ianhoughton.com

What can you do right now to make a difference within your business? Do you have a customer service member or a member of staff that deals with your customers? If you don't, should you? If you're a one-person business, a one-man band (so to speak), do you do this yourself? If you don't, well, should you? And, if you should, what should you do, and how should you do it? What comments and complaints do you see constantly happening in your industry or within your specific business? Make those notes. What can you put in place right now to make sure that all these things are being taken care of? To make sure that your customers are not going to another business that does it better, what do you need to do or change about your business?

By the way, whether you are a one-man band or employ hundreds of people, **the only person that should be in charge of ensuring this service philosophy exists and thrives within your business is YOU!!! – It's that important!**

So, just by doing this is really going to set you apart. It won't take long for customers to notice, especially if you have existing customers. And it won't take long for them to give you feedback, and for your customers to tell more people about your company, to Tweet about it, to Facebook it, and so on.

Notes:

What do other businesses do that is bad? What do other businesses do that is outstanding?

Can you find a business that offers outstanding service, if so who are they and what do they do that makes them outstanding?

Are a lot of businesses making the same common mistakes, If so, what are they?

Look at the businesses that have outstanding service. What did they do? How did they treat you? What was it that made them different?

If you just called the business on the telephone and they had outstanding service, why was it outstanding? Was it the individual you spoke to? If it was, what was it about that person?

What can you do right now to make a difference within your business?

Do you have a customer service member of staff that deals with your customers? If not, do you need one?

What comments and complaints do you see constantly happening in your industry or within your specific business?

What can you put in place right now to make sure your customer is being taken care of?

Chapter 4: Adopting and Adapting Best Practices

This is one of the biggest pieces of information I feel I can give you right now relating to service. We talked about copying, adapting and adopting. Although I might say the word copy, I'll never ever mean to rip off somebody's idea and steal it. What I mean by copying is this: **it's about becoming consciously aware of what's good and works and what's bad and doesn't work**.

As a child, when we used to go on vacation or holiday around America, Hong Kong, Thailand and Europe, and all these different places, my parents were always consciously aware of how they could continue to enhance their own business. How could they constantly make it better? I always remember, as a kid, they'd always want to make their business as good as it could possibly be. So many people become so flippant with their business that they don't even care about it. If you think about some businesses that you've dealt with, you will be able to think of instances where you felt: "This business just doesn't even care." The simple fact that you're reading this book right now is a great example that you're searching for ways to make your business better; if not ways to make your business better, better ways to make your business more profitable, the correct way with integrity.

Profit is not a bad word. It's a *great* word, but I believe it's only great when you are giving back to your customers in return. If we're just "stealing" all the time and giving nothing in return, the business can't last long. It just can't. You have to give. It has to be giving on both sides, the business and the customer. Win - win.

I have got some most bizarre stories to tell. I remember being in Disney World standing in front of a trash compound. Here I am in Disney with all these amazing characters walking around that I've loved all my life, and my parents wanted me to have my photo taken in front of the trash compound. At that time, my parents had just got the business that they still have to this day. They were looking at building a trash compound of their own, and let's be honest about it, how do you build a *nice* trash compound? How do you "dress" it up? Fortunately for them, they had seen a few examples that caught their eye, and they would look into replicating them. The trash compound at Disney caught my Dad's attention, but he didn't want to be seen as taking a picture of it. So he would just tell me: "Okay, Ian, go stand in front of the trash compound and give me a smile so I can take a photo of it."

And I'd respond: "Come on, please. Can you just take a photo of the trash compound?"

"No, no, get in front of it." He'd replied.

We'd be somewhere else in America and he would take a photograph of the floor. Or we'd be at Manchester Airport in the UK waiting to leave, and I remember my father seeing a customer suggestion box. It was almost like a podium-style and had the little cards for people to fill out. This is standard now, but it wasn't back then. It had the little cards that sat on top, a pen for customers to use, a stand to write on, and a little podium box to insert the comment cards. He took a photo of that. We'd be somewhere and we'd experienced outstanding service, he'd get a pad and make a note of what they did and how they did it.

"Oh, look what they've got. They employed one person just to do this," whatever 'this' may be. "Well, if we employed one person to do the same thing, could we get the same results?" And the answer the majority of the time was yes, we could. We could achieve exactly the same results just by paying attention to what worked and then understanding how we could adapt and adopt it into our business and then implementing it, they JFDI!

I still go places now and I still see things that I absolutely love and I just take it. If I know that it's going to benefit my business, I will take the idea. Now, I can't take it exactly as it is shown or used, because I may have seen it in a restaurant, or in a hotel, and I don't own a hotel or restaurant. However, what works, works. **If you see something that you like, take it, adapt it and adopt it into your business, in a way that benefits your business.**

How can we start to look at where to find good businesses? Well, we can find good businesses all over the world. What you want to do is look within your industry and also outside of your industry. Who is the best in your industry? Now, how do they sell what you sell? What do they do that is different? What do they do that is different that you like? What do they do that is different that you don't like? Whatever it is that you like, you can adapt it and adopt it to your business. But don't copy it exactly, because that's when you get into trouble. It's not about stealing, but about understanding best business practices, things that work, and implementing them in a way that suits your business.

If we have a business, we want to be the best. Don't we? Don't we want to be the top person in our industry? The only way we can figure out what that is or how to become the top person in our industry is to give better service and even create an outstanding experience for our customers. So, we need to look at some of the best service providers out there and adapt and adopt the way they do it into our business. Then you need to start to look at other companies that are *not* in your industry. How do they do what they do? What is it that they do that is really good? Which concept do you like? What are they trying to achieve that you think make sense and could be applied in your business? That's what you want to be looking at right now. Start to look at all these different things that you can adapt and adopt and implement within your business.

Let's look at an example: let's say you're in a store and you hear a member of the sales staff say something that you like, take it and implement it immediately within your business, JFDI. If you have a business that sells a product or service, what did you hear through another salesperson that you thought: "I would like that"? Is it something you could immediately implement within your business? If not, does it need to be tweaked? If it needs to be tweaked, how does it need to be tweaked? Where does it need to be tweaked? Keep making those notes.

You can increase the sales and the level of service in your business just by paying attention to others. That's what I do for a living. I pay attention to what goes on and then tweak it to improve my business, and I also tweak it to improve the businesses that I work with and sometimes an amazing idea can come out of it. You can look at some idea, some work plan and you can say: "Oh, I just really love that". If I did *this* I could get *that* looking like *that*." The quality of the service you provide, whatever it is that you offer, is going to go up. So, what is *it*? Get out there. Go and visit businesses within your industry. Go and visit businesses *outside* your industry. Take a notepad and a pen or take a voice recorder, and start to make notes now.

"Oh, I was in a restaurant and I saw a server totally and utterly ignored that person." Well, you want to make sure that your staff doesn't do that. So, what do you need to do? You need to make sure that your staff pays attention to the wants and needs of your customers. You need to make sure that your staff are constantly looking around to make sure the customers are not looking around for help." How many times have you been in a store and you end up walking around trying to find the salesperson? It gets frustrating.

A lot of us have cameras within our cellphones or mobile phones. We also have a notes section on the phone, and we can access emails on our phones. Now, I'll tell you one of the things I do when I come across a good idea. I do one of two things, depending on what setting I'm in. First, I'll pull my phone out and make a note of what I've seen and then email it to myself. That way, the next day it's there in my inbox, and then I reinvestigate it and I look at it and ask myself: "Okay, how can I now make this work in my business?" Second, if I'm working with another business, I'll ask myself: "How can I make what they're doing work in my clients business?"

Sometimes I'm in a place where I don't want to type or write, so I'll go into the voice recorder on my mobile/cellphone, I'll record what's on my mind, and then I'll email the recording to myself so everything is there for me to look at first thing in the morning.

So, I put it to you now. This is your business. This is your life. What are you going to do right now to find ways to increase the level of service within your business? Are you going to sit here and start to make some notes? Are you going to make some voice recordings? Are you going to get out and have a look to see what other businesses are doing in your industry, and those outside your industry? Are you going to get out of your office, walk back into your office, and try to view things through a customer's point of view?

Sometimes the hardest thing in the world is that we become stagnant within our business. You may have heard the phrase: **"You start to work *in* the business and not *on* the business."** The whole point is, as the owner of the business, to always be looking at it as a business and not to get caught up in a 9 to 5 job. I'm not saying that we shouldn't be working from 9 am to 5 pm. That's not what I'm saying at all. What I'm saying is don't become an employee of your own business. You set your business up for what reason? Whatever that reason was, what vision did you have when you wanted to start that business? Was your intention to treat your customers badly, or did you want to treat them differently and make a difference? Did you want to treat them differently and didn't know how to, or has your judgment been clouded over the period of owning that business. Sometimes we all just lose focus, that's one thing, but it's up to you now to look to see how you can increase the level of service within your business. What do others do well? What can you take from their practices, and implement in your business?

Notes:

How can you constantly make your business better?

Who is the best in your industry? How do they sell what you sell?

What do they do that is different?

What do they do that is different that you like?

What do they do that is different that you don't like?

Look at other companies that are *not* in your industry. How do they do what they do? What is it that they do that is really good? Which concept do you like?

What are they trying to achieve that you think make sense and could be applied in your business?

What can you take from their practices, and implement in your business?

Is it something you could immediately implement within your business? If not, does it need to be tweaked? If it needs to be tweaked, how does it need to be tweaked?

What are you going to do right now to find ways to increase the level of service within your business?

Are you going to get out and have a look to see what other businesses are doing in your industry, and those outside your industry?

Chapter 5: Looking After THE Customer

Being brought up, I remember asking my father if he really believed in the old saying: "**The Customer is Always Right**" I figured no one could really genuinely believe it. After some considerable thought he looked at me and said... **"Yes, I truly believe that THE customer is always right, but that A customer isn't".**

Over the years, I really dissected what he meant by this. When we set our business up, knowing that we had to have customers to survive, we realized one thing: we *must* set our business up and run it the way we believe the majority of our customers should be looked after. Many businesses get so confused when it comes to customer service and the customer, because they're trying to please every individual customer. The truth of the matter is this: you will never please *every* customer. You have to look at the customer as a whole.

So, let's say you have 100 customers. Well, you have one *whole* customer. You cater to the entire customer, so every decision you make based on your business, based on your service should be made as a whole. When businesses start to look at just the *individual* customer, this is when big mistakes happen in the business, because what is right for *one* customer is not right for another. You need to look at how you approach your business and say: "Okay, am I taking all of this information from every individual customer, getting totally confused, and achieving nothing; or am I getting totally confused and doing too much?"

When you set your business up, how did you intend to look after your customers? Make a note right now in the note section of the things *you* intended to do. What was your complaint procedure? What did you anticipate as a means to be able to pull a situation back when a complaint happened? How did you intend to look after the customer when the customer walked through the door or rang the telephone? How did you intend to follow-up with a customer after a first visit? You need to look at all of the areas of your business.

I want to talk very quickly about following up, which should be a whole section in itself. However, I'm going to mention it here because it falls right into the customer service section. Let me tell you a couple stories that I'm going through right now and how I'm noticing poor service. I'm going through these on purpose as I'm writing this book to see exactly how other businesses in different industries treat these situations.

I'm in the process of looking for health insurance. I need to get some for myself. So, about three weeks ago I contacted a company and said: "I'm looking for some health insurance." I got some prices, and all this information I needed, great. I said to the guy: "I'm really, really busy at the moment. I've got a bunch of stuff going on, would you do me a favor, keep in contact with me and force that we meet, so I can get this paperwork done and get the process started. I am here, there and everywhere. I fly to different locations, see different clients, speak at seminars including my own, help different people, plus also I'm writing books and creating video programs. There's a bunch of stuff going on in my life."

So, I set everything up with this guy for health insurance and since then, I've not heard one single thing from him. Now, he knew I wanted to do it. He knew I needed the health insurance, and that I needed to get it sorted out, so it's a very simple transaction, isn't it? Get on top of the customer, make sure all your work is done, and make the process as easy as possible for them to buy the product or service. Oh, and be sure to look after them.

I've heard nothing from this guy and I sit here and scratch my head as I'm writing this book. This was a very easy sale for him and yet he didn't follow up. He's probably doing this to other potential clients too. So, be really mindful of this. One of the biggest things you can do to increase profits is to follow up with a potential customer. Try it, you'll be surprised!

I'll give you my next thought. I own properties. I own a bunch of them, and I had a real estate agent contact me. She was an agent for my British properties, and she contacted me regarding me possibly selling one of them. Now, at this moment in time, I've got a lot of stuff going on in my life, and I'm very focused on the things I need to do. I know this might sound crazy, it might not, but I am not really *that* concerned as to whether this property sells or not. If it does, great. I'll make some money. If it doesn't, that's great too. I can still make the money anyway through the rent, but it *would* be beneficial to me if the property sold.

I emailed the real estate agent and let her know that I had a lot of things going on just then. This is what I actually put in my email: "I'm definitely interested in doing this, but I have a lot of stuff going on. It would be very helpful if you could make this as easy as possible for me. If you don't hear from me, it's not because I am not interested. It's because I've got a lot of stuff going on."

Now, to be fair I heard from her once, but it's been a couple of weeks since I heard. She might be saying: "Well, okay. He's not interested," but I definitely specifically put in the email that I *was* absolutely interested.

It's so important to understand that businesses just don't follow up with their customers or potential customers and this is part of the service process, isn't it? Of course it is. We're trying to better serve our customers. How can we better serve our customers if we're not serving them at all? In both of the examples I've mentioned, they were not serving me. They should have. I had even told them both: "I want to do this." But yet, they didn't follow up.

I tell you now; if there is a lesson you can learn from this, it is to always follow up with your customers. You don't know what's going on in their life. You don't know if their attention has been taken away by other things, by writing books, by seeing clients, by traveling a lot. They don't know what goes on in your daily life, yet they make a decision to not call, to not follow up.

Yet if someone else calls me about the same things from different businesses and they are really proactive and JFDI, they *will* get the business. Do you understand just how important this is?

Now, a word of caution... And here is something you don't expect to hear in a book about Customer Service. Lean forward I have to whisper this... *It's OK to not follow-up and get rid of some of your customers if you feel that they don't benefit your business or if they cause you problems.* You know the people I'm talking about, the ones who constantly complain, upsetting your hard working staff, late or even worse... bad payers. You know the ones I'm talking about, get rid of them.

You'll find it a wonderful and liberating experience. It's your business, you have the right to select your clients and do business with nice people.

There is a third example I want to talk about, and this one probably flaws me more than anything else. "Flaws me" is the British phrase for amazes me, knocks me down.

I am in the process of finding a new place to live. I'm very specific with the criteria that I'm looking for in my new place. I definitely don't want to rush into buying just anything, I want to rent first, and I don't want to rent a house; I want to keep my life as simple as possible. I want to keep housing as simple as possible. I'm looking for an apartment, but I have a very specific criteria. I want a nice balcony. I want to be able to watch the sunset every night, that's what I moved to America for. To enjoy the way of life here... (the sun!). I saw an apartment building that I really liked. It's a brand new apartment building, which has really contemporary units, and it looks great. It's exactly what I'm looking for. I have called this company four or five times. I've emailed them two or three times, and I've heard nothing back. Not one single thing. This is a top quality apartment complex, yet run poorly.

The simple reason that you are raising your level of conscious awareness of service in a business is that it will put you ahead of the game. You may just think: "Oh, this is just service and everybody does it." No, they don't. Most businesses do just enough to get by. They don't go above and beyond to look after you, they don't offer you outstanding levels of service. How many businesses have you noticed in your lifetime that really seem to only care about themselves? Now, think about it. Have you ever walked into a business and sometimes they can't even bother to look you in the eye? Sometimes they kind of wave their hand at you as if to say: "Shhh, I'm busy right now. I'm on the phone right now or I'm doing something I think is important," or they've been very harsh in the way that they talk to you or approach you?

www.ianhoughton.com

My eyes are wide open to this every day. Probably one of the unfortunate things of doing what I do, is this hits me like a ton of bricks every single day. Every business I come into contact with, I see massive mistakes being made all over the place. The majority of these mistakes are just related to poor service, and like I said in the previous chapters, these are all fixable. Not only are they fixable, they are free. It costs nothing to fix this stuff, but yet, we don't do it. We don't do it because we get caught up in our life. We get caught up in business and our attention gets taken away from us or maybe we just don't even care. Well, if we don't care, the customer sees it, I am a customer, I see it. I've been in small restaurants that don't look that great and received the most phenomenal service that makes me go back over and over again. I have a few little beach bars and restaurants that I go to on a regular basis. Almost a little bit like the TV program 'Cheers', where I walk in and everybody knows my name. I like that, I like the fact that they know what I like to drink. I like the fact that they know that I like my food a certain way or certain things I don't like on my food and it makes life easier for me. On the other hand I also have been into some beautiful business and received the worst service.

What people don't understand is that **everything I've just discussed can be systemized to guarantee the same experience and the same service every time**. The problem most people have in their businesses though, is that they allow the staff, or an individual member of the staff to make these decisions. Now, I'm not saying that shouldn't happen; what I'm saying is, if you have an exceptional member of your staff, find out what it is that makes them exceptional. What do they do specifically that is exceptional? Then write it down, begin to understand what they do that makes them exceptional and build a system so that every member of staff gives that level of service all the time.

You should make notes when you get good comments and good feedback from customers, when they mention something that a member of your staff has done. Become consciously aware of these things now and start to make that happen every time, every day with every member of the staff, and with every customer.

When you go into these businesses and you see that they don't care, it is blatantly obvious. They make us feel bad and at times we walk away thinking: "How are these people even in business?" Yet, they are, and the truth of the matter is that they are probably not doing that great. They might be making a ton of money, but I'll guarantee you this: they are losing a ton of money too. If a business is doing well financially and they're not looking after the customer, the dollars (or the pounds) are just flying out the door. It could be tens of thousands, it could be hundreds of thousands or it could be more, but what matters is that the money is going, and it's going because the customer found somebody else that does what that first company does, but better. A company that looks after them better, that makes them feel warm and comfortable, better than the other company; people that actually care. **Or... they just do it a little better, isn't that also scary?** *Think about business that you are possibly losing now to businesses that are doing it just a little bit better than you currently are.*

Start to look within your business and become aware of what other businesses do. Look at different members of your staff. Who is really good, and in what areas? Why are they good? What do they do specifically that's good? Continue to make notes now if you can, in the notes section. What things have you heard that are sparking off interest and attention? Things that make you say: "Oh, right. This is a good idea. I like that. I'll do that. All my customers rave about this one member of staff. I am going to pull that person in and talk to them, and I'm going to find out what they do, how they do it, why they do it, and why they think this way." Because, once you can understand all that, then you can implement what they do, can't you? And, you can make it happen all the time, and that's what it's all about. It's making good policy and procedures happen all the time. Not haphazardly, not sporadically, all the time consciously because you're now starting to get on top of your game and understand your business.

When a customer walks through the door, how do you greet them? What is the correct way to greet them? Has it been tested? A lot of businesses never test; they don't say: "This is the way we're going to do it," or: "Oh, why do you do it this way?" They may just say: "Oh, we've done it this way for thirty years," but it's not working for you. Merely saying: "I've done it for thirty years" doesn't cut the mustard. It doesn't matter, because we need to find out what *works*. We need to find out what makes that customer feel warm and comfortable all the time.

So, take some time and really think about this. Think about the businesses that you come into contact with. Think about the bad ones, think about the good ones, think about your staff, and start to make this all work together within your business.

Now think about how businesses *used* to look after their customers. You know, in the "olden days". I'm talking of back in the 20's, 30's, 40's, 50's, when they seemed to really care about the customer. Think about the old movies you've seen; the customer would walk into the business and the owner or the person working in the store would almost be waiting there for them. They would have a big smile on their face. They'd know their name. They'd know what time they were coming in, and not only that but if they were in a grocery store (for example), or a butchers or a bakers, they would probably even have their order ready for them in a nice little basket. And not only did they have the food ready in the basket, but that big smile that greeted them when they walked through the door. And they actually took some time and genuinely cared about the customer and would talk to them about life. It was their time they put aside just to talk, just build that friendship and customer relationship.

In fact, that's part and parcel to what Disney does now. Think about that, Disney builds customers by merely harking back to an almost forgotten era! Their cast members (what they call employees) are trained to put customer service and satisfaction ahead of profits. Why? Because they know that doing so will bring profits in the long run. Happy and loyal guests are the kind of people who spend money, and tell others about what an outstanding experience they had at Disney World.

With the companies back in the "old days", some of them may not have realized that's what they were consciously doing. Whether they knew it or not, they were doing it, and they were building that loyalty with the customer. Not only that, they might even have a bone or a bowl of water for the dog the customer had with them, or a lollipop for their child. You know, these are the things that have low to no cost for us to do; yet, so many businesses don't do them.

This is where you start to look at how we can give a customer an amazing experience by really looking after them through our customer service. Then again, why would they want to go anywhere else? And especially, as we said, in an economy like today business is a little bit tougher, and we're all trying to find the edge. A lot of us try to find the edge by going out there to try to find new customers all the time, but what we fail to realize is that the majority of our money will come from the existing customers we already have if we look after them correctly.

You may have heard of the 80/20 rule. 80% of your profits come from 20% of your customers. Therefore, let's find out who our 20% customers are and let's look after them really well. 80% of the results you produce is created by 20% of the effort you put into it. So, we really need to look at where we are most productive. Not only where we are most productive but, what can we do to somebody to give them this phenomenal experience of dealing with us as a business? There are things that don't cost much to do. Yet, they can be seen as one of the nicest things you can do for a customer and trust me they will remember it.

It's about thinking differently. It's about trying to come away from the game a little bit. The game of 'business', the game of our industry. Taking a step back and saying: "What can we do that's different? What can we do that breaks the mold within our industry and we can do this easily by going out and trying to see what other industries do. Something that we can adapt and adopt to our business?" It's about implementing that, JFDI. It's about doing it in a way that increases the customer service. And if we can, it's about increasing and improving the experience of doing business with us.

So, take some time, go out, open your eyes, and be consciously aware of things going on around you. Next time you go to a restaurant, have a look at the way they do things. The next time you are in a store, just look at the way you're dealt with. Are you able to say to yourself: "Well, I like the way they did that. Well, I *didn't* like the way they did that." If you didn't like the way they did it, what was it about what they did that you didn't like? And then make sure that you're *not* doing it. If there was something you saw that you did like, what was it and is there a way of putting that into your business? Is there a way of making sure that your customer gets that every time they deal with you as opposed to now and again?

Notes:

When you set your business up, how did you intend to look after your customers?

What things did *you* intend to do. What was your complaint procedure? Do you have one?

Are you taking different feedback from every individual customer and getting totally confused, and achieving nothing? Are you getting totally confused and doing too much?

How did you intend to look after the customer when the customer walked through the door or rang the telephone?

How did you intend to follow-up with a customer after a first visit?

If you have an exceptional member of your staff, find out what it is that makes them exceptional. What do they do specifically that is exceptional?

When you get good comments from customers, great feedback and they mention something that a member of your staff has done or something that happened, what was it?

What staff do you have that are really good, and in what areas? Why are they good? What do they do specifically that's good?

What things have you heard that are sparking off interest and attention? Who are your top 20% customers?

Chapter 6: The Impact of Staff on Customer Service

Do you know for sure that you have the correct staff, and not only the correct staff but the correct staff in the correct *places*? You always want to 'Employ for attitude and teach skill'.

I accept that there are certain businesses where skills must come with the job. For example, if you are a lawyer and you're bringing in a new partner, then obviously they must be trained as a lawyer. But, at the same time, what's absolutely crucial to really making this all work, to really have this all come together is to make sure that you have the right staff (or partners) and they have the right attitude. There's nothing worse, and I've seen this before in businesses, than having a great member of staff who is very good at their job yet, has a real negative attitude. I've seen it before. I've even dealt with it in my family's businesses. You can often see a member of staff being very good at their job; however the problem is that their attitude stinks. Then you get caught in what can only be called a no-win situation. You think: "I can't let this person go. They carry so much weight. They do so much for me." Yet, what we don't realize is that they're the ones that actually hold us back. I know you'll read this now and realize that you're in this situation yourself, or you have been in it in the past. If you haven't, trust me, it will come about one day.

I've been in situations before where I've had a manager that I felt I couldn't let go because they carried so much weight. But, at the same time, in the back of my mind, I knew that they really weren't the right person. The crazy thing was, the longer I left it, the worse it got. What was even crazier than that was when I did let go of them, the whole business totally changed. It became much easier, and it was easy to find somebody that could do the job that that person was previously doing.

Yet, we get caught up in a situation and we can't "cut the cord" and get rid of someone who is a millstone around our company's neck. What we can't do is have a member of staff that brings the team down. You know your business is a team effort. If you are a "one man band" working from home, there's nothing wrong with that. I actually kind of like to live my life that way; I like things as simple as possible, as little staff as possible. But, it's important to make sure we have the right staff in the right places and that we have the people with the good attitude out in front of the customers, because they're the people we want in that position. We definitely don't want to be bringing our bad attitude people out front, do we?

So, really, take some time and look at that, and say to yourself: "Is there a member of staff that's holding the business back right now? Is there somebody I'm too scared to let go of because I think they do too much, and I think I'm not going to be able to replace them?" Yet, deep down you know that they're realistically bringing your business down. I'm not saying it's an easy decision to come to, but I'm saying that once you make the decision you'll look back on it and say: "I can't believe I didn't do that earlier."

So, what do you expect from your staff? What are your expectations? And more to the point, I know this might sound a crazy one now, do your staff even know what you expect of each of them?

There are so many businesses that I work with, and when I have a chance to speak to the staff, they say, "We don't really know what we're meant to do, what is expected of us." Most of the top companies let their staff know what is expected.

Your staff should know what you expect of them, what they ought to be doing and achieving, but also what they shouldn't be doing. **Take some time and let your staff know what can get them fired.** Allow them to be very clear on it. So, let's say for example, the owner of the business turns to the staff and says: "Look, you're not going to get fired for making a mistake, so don't be scared about making one. What you'll get fired over, is making a mistake and not telling me, and allowing it to get totally out of control."

It's not the fact that they make a mistake. We all make mistakes and, in fact, we want to embrace those mistakes because they are just somebody saying to us: "Okay, that's something you don't know enough about, and that's why the mistake happened. So now, go and get the knowledge you need on it; go learn about it, and systemize it to make sure it doesn't happen again." But you can't punish a member of staff because most of the time you might not know how to do it yourself either.

Your staff need to be aware of what can get them fired because it will allow them to settle into their jobs quicker and be the best they can be for you. Your job as the owner is to support the staff, to take care of them, to nurture them, to help guide them. They're coming to you. They're looking up at you saying: "Please show me the way. Show me what I need to do. Show me how I can be better at my job to make you happier." As much as staff members love cash incentive bonuses, they also really, really appreciate equally as much being noticed, getting a pat on the back. The business owner just walking up and saying "You know what? I want to thank you for what you did there. I really appreciate it. I saw the effort you made and I want to say thank you because you did what was right for this business. You went above and beyond for the customer. You gave them outstanding service and you gave them an experience too."

If I asked you to draw up a chart showing the hierarchy within your business my guess is it would look something like this:

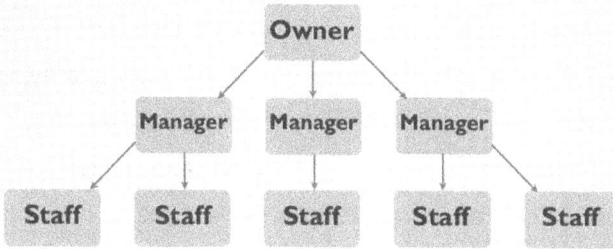

But how about changing the usual perspective... Consider the following:

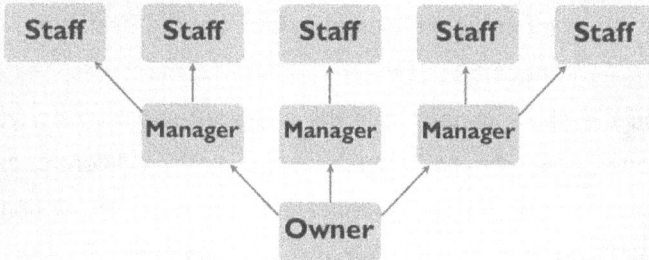

With the more senior staff giving support and help to those on the "front line"

Commend them for good actions. **Reprimand in private, praise in public.** Never reprimand staff in public. It is one of the worst things you could possibly do. It's totally and utterly unacceptable and it's totally and utterly unprofessional. Always, if they need to be reprimanded, it needs to be done in private. They don't need to be made a spectacle of. However, if they do something great, then praise them in public. Let other people see what that employee did to earn that praise, let them feel how nice it feels that you noticed what they did. It'll go a long way with your staff and at the end of the day we're trying to get our staff into a peak performance mindset so they can perform better for us and therefore perform better for our customers. You need to come to a decision as to how you're going to embrace looking after customers, giving them outstanding service, and starting to improve their experiences doing business with you. Because if you do, the next thing you need is to come from a thinking point of doing whatever it takes to serve the customer.

Remember we mentioned before that the customer is a whole. If you have 50 customers and they come to you and all tell you the same thing that is *the* customer speaking. If you have one or two coming to you saying something different, that doesn't mean that we change everything we've previously done, does it? It means we're going to pay attention to the masses, to the whole, to the bulk of our customers. So, when we work with our staff, we need to let them know we've taken on this philosophy of giving the customer outstanding service and an outstanding experience. We need to let the members of staff know that this philosophy is doing whatever it takes to get the customer taken care of correctly. Whatever it takes to make a customer say: "Wow, that was amazing. That was unbelievable.

80

That was an amazing piece of service I just got there." Or: "That was an amazing experience I just got at that company." **The more intense the experience the better the experience; the more chance you've got of that customer coming back**, especially if you're really good at what you do. You see, you might be really good at what you do right now and are scratching your head saying: "Well, I don't understand this. How am I really good at what I do, yet I just don't seem to be having the breakthroughs?" Well, it's time to talk to your customers, isn't it? It's time to ask them: "How do you perceive me and my business? Am I doing a good job by looking after you?" Then listen to what the customer as a whole says.

Notes:

What do you expect from your staff?

Do your staff even know what you expect of each of them?

Is there a member of staff that's holding the business back right now? Is there somebody you're too scared to let go of because you think they do too much, and you think you're not going to be able to replace them?

Chapter 7: Keeping Constant Contact With the Customer

How many times in your life have you been in the process of buying something or showing interest in something and yet, you get very little contact or communication from that business after?

Now, I know as a business owner you are caught between a rock and a hard place because part of you thinks: "I don't want to bother my customer too much," and then the other part of your brain says: "Yeah, but I need to get the business too". There is no harm in keeping in contact with the customer. In fact, the more contact you keep with the customer, the more you're at the forefront of their brain, so the moment they want to buy something, you're the one they think of because you're the one that has kept in communication with them.

A study was done that said you have to be in front of a customer 14 times before they even notice that you're there; I'm sure you have seen this yourself. If you're driving, especially more so in America than the UK, there are big billboards. Now, why do the billboards work? Well, you don't necessarily pay attention to them all the time. Okay, you might look at them, you might notice them, but you're probably not really paying attention to the message on them. But, over a period of time you actually consciously become aware of their message.

The point of it is, you need to be in front of the customer when they are ready to take action. If you've been there long enough and you've built an outstanding relationship with them, they are going to want to come and buy from you. To keep in contact with a customer is not just about trying to keep selling to them all the time. It's about offering them service, offering up your knowledge so you can educate the customer to keep their taste buds tingling, so when they are in that period that they want to buy, *you* are the one that has fed them knowledge, fed them information and continued to educate them, and they will want to come and buy from you.

Think of it as the lifetime value of the customer. Keep in contact with your customers. Let them know that you are still thinking about them. If this is a new customer that you are trying to pull in, like I said, educate them. Send them emails, send them videos, send them audio programs, send them mail outs, send them newsletters telling them: "This is what is going on. This is the new news, the new information that we have just received and we want to pass it on to you." Now, if it is complicated or confusing information, put it in layman's terms for them. What does it mean to *them*?

www.ianhoughton.com

If you are in an industry that is very complicated or complex, try to make yourself look not too big. Make yourself look caring, and put the information about your company in terms that are beneficial to the customer. "Hey, we just want to let you know that this new product has just been released and what that means is it's easier for end users, it has been streamlined, and now they are able to do this". Whatever the benefits are, that's where you fill in the blanks, so to speak. Here's an example: "We have just received notification that Ford is bringing out a new vehicle and it is going to have better fuel efficiency. We just learned of this, and we wanted to let you know. We will keep you updated."

It's not just about the sales process either. Again, it's not just about getting the initial sale from the customer. It's about being able to say: "Okay, we want to keep that customer all the time." So, it's also working with them. How many times have you dealt with a business where you are waiting to hear from them about something and they say: "The moment we find out about it, we will be in touch?" Days can go by. Sometimes even weeks, and you are sitting there saying: "Well, what the hell is going on? I have not heard from anyone in ages. Have they forgotten about me?" Although you are in the business and you may have been working on the information for the client every day for however many days, or maybe even weeks, the customer can't see that. The customer does not know. The customer *will* know however, if you pick up the phone and call them and say: "Hey, I just want to let you know, I have been working on this, and although I don't have any updated information right now, I wanted to let you know that we are still working on it. We have not forgotten about you". You see how stupidly simple something like that is? Yet, to a customer, how powerful is that?

It really tells the customer that you care; it lets the customer know that you are thinking about them, that you are going the extra mile. Here's a great example. Lawyers or solicitors in the UK often let themselves down. This is something that, when I work with lawyers I definitely bring to the forefront of their minds, and that I can speak from personal experience dealing with them, that communication with their clients is often very poor. So, if we want to differentiate ourselves as a lawyer, what is one of the easiest things that we can possibly do? We can communicate better with our customers. Send them a quick email saying: "I want to let you know I have been looking at your file today and I just wanted to get you an update. As it turns out, there is no new information to give you at the moment". Well, isn't it better to receive that email than to sit there and go: "Hum, I wonder if they even think about me? I wonder if they are even looking at my file anymore?"

Granted, I accept that lawyers have a lot of work to do, but it doesn't mean an email can't be sent out. It doesn't mean they can't put a note on their computer to notify them every three days, a week, whatever they choose. For that matter, they could just assign an assistant to send out an email to update the client. The assistant could just look at the client's file, look at any updated information, and keep in contact with the customer. "I want to let you know we have looked at your file today. This piece of information has come in, which means that your case (your project, whatever) is moving forward," or: "I want to let you know I just looked at your file and there is no new information. However, I did notice that we should be getting some information in a couple of days. I will keep you updated."

If you have a car and you take it to a garage, maybe there is something that has gone wrong with it, you take the vehicle in, and then you don't hear anything. You may ask them: "Have you finished with it? Have you got the part? Have you *not* got the part for it? Where are we at with it?" You end up calling and calling, and you leave voicemails and you never get calls returned. If you run a car dealership right now, you are listening to this and saying: "Well, that is terrible." That means you are ahead of the game because that is how most people are. It is all about caring, it is about going the extra mile.

It is about keeping in contact with the customer, because you do not know when the customer is going to buy. They may buy from you again immediately, they may not. It might be a large purchase, which means it takes more time to think about, rather than going to buy a sandwich. It doesn't mean that even if you own a sandwich store you can't give outstanding service. It doesn't mean we can't give an experience every time they buy a sandwich from us, because of course we can. The best things in life are free. *Service is free, an experience is free.*

You need to constantly be adding value to the lives of your customers. **You want to be what I call a value-factorer. That means, you add value.** You want to be one of those businesses that the customers receive information from an email, a phone call, a letter, direct mail, a newsletter, and you want them to say, "Great, what am I going to learn about now?" If you are in an industry, you should have a passion and a love for what you do. You absolutely should, and if you do, then make sure that passion spills over to your customers. Why do you do the things you do? Why do you love what you love? There is information that goes on in your mind on a daily basis, and on a second basis your customers would love to get that knowledge. They would just love to know a little bit more about what you know. So, what information can we put together, what little videos? You may think: "Well, I really don't know that much." I will guarantee you do. I guarantee that some of the smallest, tiniest little things that you feel are totally irrelevant are hugely relevant to your customers.

If you are a hairdresser, how do you do the things you do? How do you cut hair? What do you look at when you cut hair? What do you look for? Do you look at a customer and build their hair around their face? Do you look at the way their hair lays before you cut it? What do you do? Educate the customer. I know you might be thinking right now: "Well, this is crazy, and no customer wants to know how I cut hair". I will guarantee you, if you offer them an experience; they do, because you keep teaching them. When you teach others, they take the information, and they too teach others. So, it doesn't just stop for you. You might think: "Yes, but everybody in my industry knows that". Okay, great. But how many people in your industry are actually educating the customer? Most people don't. Most people don't see the relevance in it. It's building such a strong bond between you and the customer; it is showing them that you have outstanding service. You are educating them and giving them an experience, and when they are in the position that they want to buy, they will come to you. So, all this stuff needs to be really thought about.

Hopefully you have had a couple of "aha" moments here and hopefully you are able to really look at your business and say: "What areas can I now look at improving? What areas do I know about, that I can share with my customers and keep in contact with my customers concerning? I need to give them an experience. I need to let them know that if I am working on their file. They will not sit at home or sit by the telephone and wait for it to ring for an update". There is nothing worse than that. **If a customer is calling you it is because you have left it too long to contact them.**

Notes:

How often do you keep in touch with your customers? How often should it be?

Do you educate your customer?

Do you let them know why you do the things you do?

Do you let them know why you love what you love?

Chapter 8: OW!!! Into a Wow!!!

This is one of the biggest things I ever learned about in customer service. An OW into a WOW explodes customer service, blows it out of the water, and this is when we start to talk about the customer experience.

I mention this a few times throughout the book, but really, we want to create an experience of doing business with you. So, what are the basics of an OW into a Wow? Well, let me make this really simple for you. An OW is when a customer has received bad service or they have received negativity from your business. Something has happened that has upset them. A complaint, the product is not right, whatever it might be. It might

91

be the fact that you have not kept in contact with them long enough or frequently enough. So an OW is when they are dissatisfied with your business. It's so important to be aware of this. If you are consciously aware of this, you can now start to make changes in your business, and this one thing could totally turn around your business. **If you have dissatisfied customers right now, you can immediately utilize what I am about to teach you and start to really turn these customers into raving fans.**

So, let's say that a customer has a set of expectations of what they are to receive from you when it comes to service. As a customer, we know enough about various industries and know the type of service we can expect when we visit a specific type of business. We have a good idea of how we are likely to be treated when we go to a lawyer's office, when we go to a restaurant, when we go to a corner store for a sandwich, or even when we go to a bar. We have pretty much set expectations of the type of service we are likely to receive, and the OW occurs when the experience does not meet our expectations.

Let's imagine those expectations a straight line. Now, when we receive an OW, we are dissatisfied, something annoys us, upsets us, and makes us go: "OW, I am not happy".

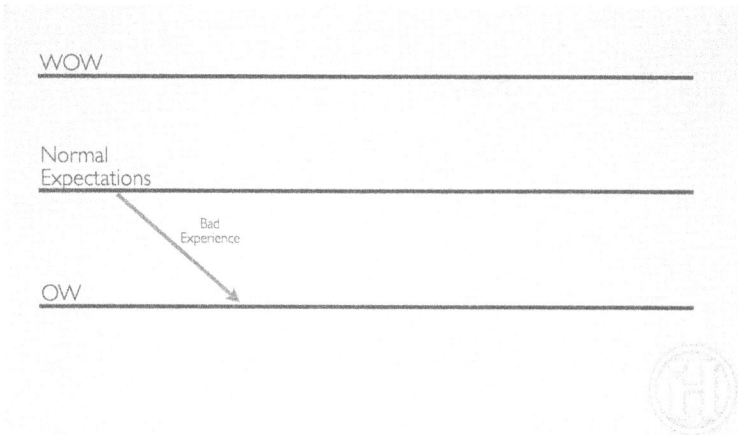

Most businesses, at best, will try to rectify the problem, and will then try to take you back to the level line. This is the service you expected to receive from them in the first place. Let's say you walked into a restaurant and they sat you at a dirty table. That is not what your set expectations were. You expected to sit at a nice clean table, but nevertheless, they sat you at a dirty table. "OW, I am upset, I am not happy". Most businesses will take you back to the straight parallel line, which means the restaurant will move you from that dirty table to a clean one. Boom, done.

WOW

Normal
Expectations

Bad
Experience

What most
Businesses do

OW

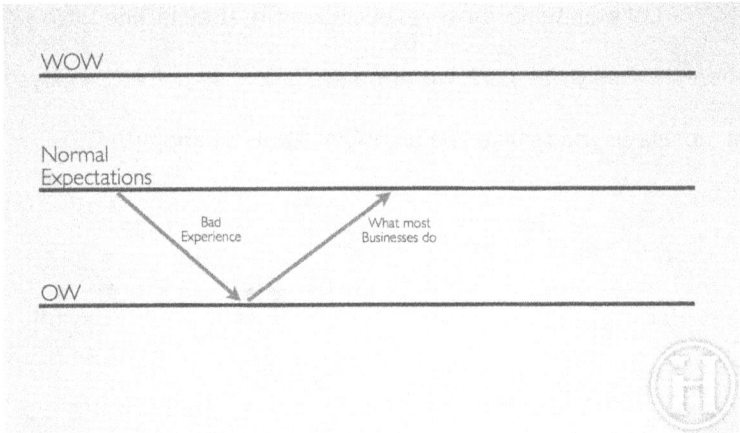

Now, most businesses end things right there. They take you right back to that level line. Now, the WOW comes when we take customers' experience above that straight line. So, you take them from an OW to a WOW. They drop below the line, they come back to the line, and then we take them above the line. We peak, and at that point, this is when we have an opportunity of showing the customer just how good we really are. If something bad has happened in your business and you have an OW, you now want to embrace this OW as an amazing opportunity to give the customer a WOW. You want to blow them out of the water and make them say: "That was unbelievable. I just had really bad service, but they went above and beyond, and I got the most amazing service I've ever had."

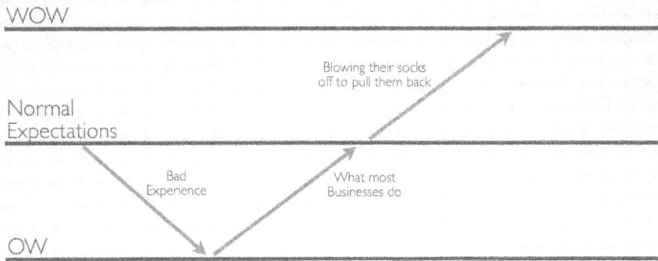

To give you an example, here is something that comes to mind from when I was a kid working in my family business. We had someone who'd had their clothes washed in the laundry and the washing machine broke down with their clothes inside. The lady came in very upset, her clothes soaking wet, and she couldn't get them out of the washing machine because it had locked up on her. Now, it wasn't our fault, because we didn't own the washing machine. We had a company that put the machines in and we split the sales 50/50. However this was our customer, so we took responsibility for it.

We can't just sit around and do as most businesses do. Most will say: "Well, that section's got nothing to do with us. You need to call the company, and they'll come down and get

95

her clothes out and give them back". That's what most businesses would do, or certainly a very large percentage of businesses.

But instead, we went in, we removed the clothes from the washer machine, and we took them to a dry-cleaners. We got the clothes cleaned and we brought them back to the lady's home. They were all nicely folded on the table so she would see them as soon as she walked in. Not only that, but there was a bottle of wine, a small box of chocolates, and some flowers with a handwritten note to top it off.

You see now, most people would never go to that extent, and let's be honest, how much did that really cost us? How much did it really cost us to not only retain the customer, but to blow them out of the water by giving them an experience of: "I was just expecting my clothes to be returned". That was her straight line; that was her level of expectation. "I expected to get my clothes back", is what she thought. She might not have expected to get them back dry-cleaned. She might have expected to get them back in a bag, soaking wet. I know everybody has slightly different levels of expectations, but we didn't do that. We went above and beyond and it cost us very, very little. But the story got told all over the resort, and we became famous in our resort because our washing machine had died. We turned what was a bad situation into an incredibly positive situation. It was about doing something different.

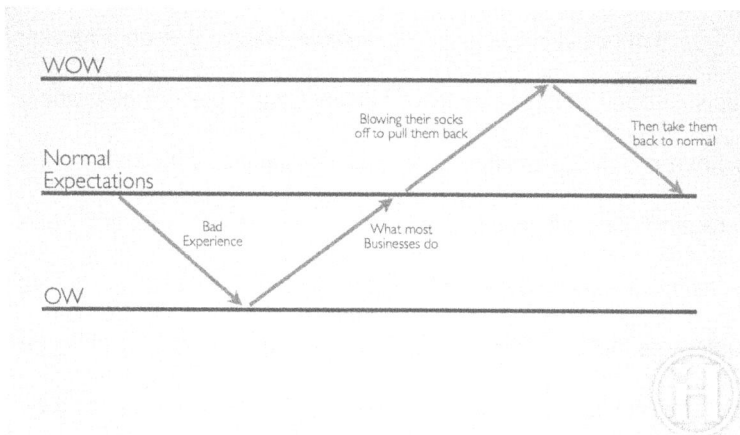

We were consciously aware of what we were doing back then. **We embraced mistakes.** When something happened, we looked at it and we would say: "Okay, here we go. Now we have an opportunity to show that customer just how good we really are". As time goes by and you start to give your customers outstanding service, and they then start to expect this from you, another strategy can come into play... If you're really, really clever at what you do, you can force an "OW"... You can make an "OW" happen on purpose to give them the WOW to show them how good you are. You can purposely make a mistake - a small one of course - to allow you an opportunity to give them a WOW experience and turn them back into raving fans again.

www.ianhoughton.com

I'm not saying we want to go out and do this on a regular basis. I don't necessarily advocate that we force our customers to have a bad experience, but what I'm saying is it can be done to remind our customers how good we are. Most of us just need to focus on the basics right now, which are just giving our customers outstanding service. What I'm saying is that when you start to come close to mastering outstanding service, then you can really give your customers outstanding 'blow your socks off' service. The important thing is that every time something bad happens in your business, embrace it and turn that OW into a WOW; turn that customer into a raving fan that just can't stop singing your praises. They are the customers that you want. They are the customers that will be loyal to you because you have shown that you care. You've gone the extra mile.

Notes:

What customers do you have that are currently unhappy at this moment?

What can you do to turn the situation around?

Do you currently offer 'WOW' experiences?

Are all your staff aware of this?

List a number of bad things that can happen within your business and how you can turn them into 'WOW' experiences.

OW!!! into a WoW!!!

Chapter 9: Going the Extra Mile

So many businesses do just enough to get by. They will do just enough to make the sale. Think about a time when you got into a store to buy something you had wanted for a long time, almost looking forward to the day. Yet, when you got there, you were let down because the process did not live up to your expectations. You thought: "Well, that happened quicker than I wanted it to," or: "They didn't really care about me that much."

When you always go the extra mile, when you become known for going the extra mile and known for giving such quality of service, I truly believe that the universe repays you back for that. I believe the universe will pay individuals and businesses back that make a difference, that break the mold, and that change the way things are done by becoming innovators.

If you always go the extra mile, you will be paid back for it. Your customers will notice. They will spread the word. So, the next time you are in your business, look at different areas and say: "Okay, what can I do here right now that breaks the mold?" Look at how you currently run your business. Look at what the industry norm is. Once you recognize and understand what the norm is, you'll be able to say: "Oh, I notice that every sandwich shop sells its food this way". Okay, stop doing it that way. What is a better way of doing it? Now, it might be something you noticed in a restaurant. It might be something you noticed from at a *dry-cleaner*. Yes, you read that right, a dry-cleaner. It doesn't matter what the business is, because you can adopt and adapt anything to your business. Anything we believe is beneficial, that is going to make our business more successful, we can adopt and adapt. So, start looking at different ways that you can go above and beyond, ways that you can go the extra mile for your customer.

Take some time and look at the different areas within your business that you feel you can elongate that process to give customers a positive experience in doing business with you. Do something for your customer that makes them feel that extra little bit special. Take just a few more minutes with them than anybody else would do. Don't try and move customers on, the way so many other businesses do.

A great example would be if there was a new housing development. You walk in to look at buying a house and they probably see a lot of customers every single day. The result? You get the standard *sub*-standard treatment. Sometimes when we deal with a large volume of customers we become very blasé about how we interact with them, and how we want to deal with these customers. Yet, if you treat every customer as being special, if you go above and beyond and treat them like they are the first customer of the day, like they are the one and only customer of the day, you will make them feel special. It's about making your customer feel special, isn't it?

How do you feel when you go somewhere and you are made to feel special? Would you walk away and go: "I didn't liked that"? Would you go: "Oh, I will never go back to that business ever again"? Of course you wouldn't say that. You are going to go back to someone that makes you feel special. You are going to go back to somewhere that every time you have dealings with them, you know that they go above and beyond. They go the extra mile.

Think of businesses that you have dealt with that you had outstanding experiences from. Businesses that maybe the owner actually takes the time to pull you to the side and talk to you one on one. What things can you look at within your business that you could make some *small* changes that a customer would *massively* see? Because, I guarantee you, there are so many areas in your business where you can go the extra mile, where you can give them that extra service, that extra support, that extra smile, that extra knowledge. The extra time that other people in your industry just don't give.

Again, what are the industry standards? What is the norm within your industry? Break the norm. Break it! Don't stay in the norm. The norm is suffocating. The norm is stifling. **The norm holds you back.** Why do you want to be held back in your business? Didn't you buy or create your business to make a profit? Did you set your business up to become at least profitable so it could pay for your life, a house, your car, the children, your vacations? Surely you didn't go into business just to make enough money to pay your bills and then sit down and worry about where your next money is coming from.

So, it is really about finding out how you can break the norm in your industry. There have been multiple examples so far in this book that you can look at and you can say: "Well, okay. Let me investigate this. I am in the (for example) retail clothing business. Let me go and have food in this restaurant, and let me just see how they treat customers when customers walk through the door. How do they greet them? Are they actually paying attention to the customer? Are they providing that special attention?" "Where would you like to sit? Would you like to be by the window? Would you like to be by the fire? We've got the sun setting at the moment?" Or: "Are you dining with us this evening? If you are, you will definitely want to sit by the window because the sun is going to be going down shortly and the sunset is going to be absolutely beautiful."

Think about how stupidly simple it was. Yet, these attentions can have a massive, positive impact on customers, making them feel different, special, noticed, recognized, significant, cared about and more importantly make them **want** to come back!

There are so many things, so many areas in your business that right now you can give an amazing piece of service, that you can attach the service to a fantastic experience - a fantastic, positive experience. Take some time and think about how all that could work.

Notes:

What is the norm in your industry about how they serve their customers?

In what ways can you go above and beyond for your customer? Do you make your customers feel special? If so, how?

What things can you look at within your business that you could make some *small* changes that a customer would *massively* see?

Are your staff actually paying attention to the customer? Are they providing that special attention?

Are you providing an amazing experience of doing business with you? What are you doing to create an experience?

Chapter 10: Quality Control

The best way for me to explain what quality control is, is to use the example of 'Hell's Kitchen', which is a TV program by Gordon Ramsey. You may or may not have seen it, but let me explain the concept very quickly: he pulls in members of the public that work within the food industry, and they have an opportunity of competing and winning a Chef position and running one of Gordon Ramsey's restaurants.

Now, as the program goes on, you will see that, when they are in the middle of a dinner service, Gordon Ramsey always stands in the front. He always stands at what he calls 'The Pass'. The whole point of him standing there (relating purely to business) is because that is his final say; that's where he now puts his stamp of approval on every single thing that leaves his kitchen (his business), to go to the customer. Yet, there are many times that you will see on the show that he will end up losing his temper because somebody will bring a substandard product to him. What he gets upset about is not just the fact that they brought this substandard product to him, it's the fact that, if he missed it, if Gordon Ramsey missed it, it would make *him* look bad. How could Gordon Ramsey allow that to leave his kitchen? This is why he becomes so frustrated and so annoyed, because that is *his* stamp of approval. The reason I have explained it this way is I need you to think about your business in that way. You need to think about your business as a kitchen. You need to make sure that you have quality control set up in your business. Before a "dish" leaves your "kitchen," you need to be sure it meets your high level of quality.

If you are a car dealer, you have a PDI, a Pre Delivery Inspection. Before that car gets delivered to the customer, you will run through a checklist to make sure that that car is perfect and that all the things that *need* to be completed *are* completed.

The gas (petrol) has been topped off, the car is nice and clean, both inside and out, all the electrics are working, and everything is right for the customer to pick up their new car. Now, we might say: "Well, that is obvious." Yet, if we own a dry-cleaner or a sandwich shop, or a corner store or a lawyer's office or a steel company, what is our quality control?

Quality control is one of the easiest ways to stabilize your business, because really that is what it is. **Quality control is stabilizing the business, stabilizing the way in which the product or service gets handed over to the customer all the time.**

So, how should it be done? What is the correct way of doing it in your business? Have you ever even written down exactly what should be done and how it should be done? If you haven't, go to the notes section right now. How should your product or service be handed over? And is it being handed over the same way every single time? Or do you have one member of the staff that does it one way and another one who does it another way, which causes inconsistency? We want consistency within our business, don't we? We don't want to be inconsistent because inconsistency means that we don't really know what we are doing. One minute it is good and the next minute it is bad. That, right there, is the difference between subconsciously doing something and consciously doing something.

That goes back to my example of the two golfers. One knows how to fix it, the other one doesn't. It's about becoming consciously aware as to how we want our product or service to be handed over every single time. How do we want our customers to be dealt with every single time? There should be a system in place.

What is a system? A system is a checklist.

Growing up, I worked in a health club. I had to be there at a certain time and I had a checklist to follow. "At this time, you open the door. At this time, you go and turn the pool lights on. At this time, you take the pool test. At this time, you turn the sauna on. At this time, you turn the Jacuzzi on. At this time, you turn the steam room on. At this time, you go into the gym and you clean the equipment, and you clean the equipment with these products, this way..."

I am not trying to be harsh here, but it was done to take 'stupid out of the equation'. Sometimes stupid things happen and those are the most frustrating things. **So, let's take 'stupid out of the equation' and let's build a system that is fool proof.** What should the employees wear? What should they say? How and where should they stand? How should their hair be styled? How should they be greeting clients? Build it around a system. Make that work.

If you have had your business for a number of years, when you started, you probably said: "Well, this is how I am going to do it. This right here is exactly how I am going to run my business". Over time, as we all know, life and business get in the way and it makes us lose focus on what is important.

So, looking back, when you first went into that business, how did you want it run? What were the visions you had? Are you doing it right now or not? Make a list. Go to the notes section right now and make a list of how you wanted the things in your business to be run. Make sure that you take the time to say: "Okay, right. How do I want this to be?"

Once you have your full list, then you need to look at it and ask yourself: "Where am I going to start?" Remember that old saying: "How do you eat an elephant? One bite at a time, just one bite". Do the first thing first. List them all, and as you do each one, cross it off. Then move on to the next one. Cross it off, and then move on to the next one. Cross it off. Are you starting to see a pattern here? Are you starting to see how this all works together? It's not complicated. It's not difficult, because none of this is.

The speed of implementation is what I like to call: "JFDI" – Just F**** Do It.** Don't mess around. Don't hang on to the information. The information that you have is of no use to anyone if you keep it to yourself. The knowledge about me putting this out there is of no use to you, no use to me, if it is not being done – if it is not being *used*. It's only relevant and useful if you are actually doing it.

And remember, when you finally do this, when you finally start to look at how you can go above and beyond, how you can break the norm in the industry, the customers will notice. The customers will keep coming back to you because you are outstanding at what you do. You give them outstanding service. You give them an outstanding experience and the customers will reward you financially for that and they will want to keep coming back to you over and over again, and that is what we want. We want to build a business where our customers love us. A business where we care about them as much as they care about us, and if we don't, then we need to. We need to start to care, because it is when we start to get into that mindset of pushing the boundaries, of breaking our industry norms, of redefining what is important to us and our business that the customers will always come back to us.

The question is, why wouldn't they? If a customer is coming to you for something and you give them outstanding service and a great product, and you go above and beyond with your experience, with your service, why would they want to go anywhere else? Seriously, why would they? Would you? And yet, sometimes we get so trapped in working in the business that we really forget to see how the business should run, and we forget to work on the business. Yet, it is by working on the business that we can start to become consciously aware of mistakes and we can fix them and we can make sure that they don't happen again.

I know that listening to what I am saying right now, this has to be resonating with you. Nothing that I am saying here is groundbreaking, or earth shattering, but it is real and honest. Isn't it? It is truthful. It is no bull. Yet, these are the things that have massive impact on the customers and we want to make life as easy as possible, as simple as possible for the customers; so let's really get down to what matters, and that is looking after the customer.

www.ianhoughton.com

Notes:

What is your quality control?

How should your product or service be handed over the your customer? Is it being done the same way all the time?

Do you have a system for all areas of your business?

How would you, in an ideal world, want your business to run, step by step? What was the vision you had? Are you doing it right now or not?

Chapter 11: The Lifetime Value of a Customer

I touched on this very briefly in a previous chapter. The lifetime value of a customer is the amount of money they can give to you over the period of time that you have them. Now, many businesses out there are only interested in the initial sale the customer brings them. They often fail to realize that the customer can continue to be a customer for years to come. We talked briefly before about the 80/20 rule. That 80% of your profits come from just 20% of your customers. So, if we knew who were the top 20% of our customers, shouldn't we pay real attention to them?

80% of your work only creates 20% of the results, and your profits. Yet, 20% of the work creates 80% of the results – and likewise the profits. So, shouldn't we find out what we are good at doing and stick to that; then find the things we are not quite so good at doing, and delegate that to somebody else?

It's important to look at and understand that true wealth really comes from the longevity of your relationships with individual customers. Think now, if you bought a car from a dealership, and let's just use Mercedes as an example. You might have gone out and maybe bought your first Mercedes. Now, you will get two types of dealers/dealerships. You have one where they make the sale. They are very happy that they made the sale, but that's where the relationship ends. When buying your *next* car, you may decide to go to a *different* dealer. But then there is the second type of dealers where they maintain the relationship through good service and regular communication. I am sure there are some of you reading this that have bought cars from the same dealer.

It really is about looking at how many times that customer can buy products from us. Realistically, if I am selling a sandwich, how many times is that customer likely to come back? How often are they likely to want to eat? Well, we need to eat, don't we? So, their chances of coming back to us again are very high based on three conditions: having a good product, having good service, and continuing to give them an experience each time. I mean, that's a no brainer, isn't it? Yet, there are so many businesses - I would think probably this is one of the biggest things that frustrates me the most - that have owners with cocky and arrogant attitudes. Some business owners just don't care.

When I lived in a certain part of America, I used to go to a particular restaurant; the food there was excellent. It was an Italian restaurant, and it had very, very good food. The restaurant was really nice, really well decorated, a beautiful restaurant. The staff were probably substandard in their training, and the owner was an absolute... let's find a nice word. He was totally and utterly arrogant. So much so, that it forced me to stop going to that restaurant because I couldn't stand to see this guy. What he didn't realize was that he lost me; he lost a customer that would have gone back once, sometimes twice a week, and brought family, friends and clients. That is 6 to 8 times a month I potentially would have gone to that restaurant, but I chose not to.

Let's say my average bill for a visit to the restaurant was around $100. So, each time I went, they got $100 from me. If it worked out I was there between 6 to 8 times a month, that is $600 to $800 a month that I would have spent there, and that they are now not getting. They are not getting it from me because the owner was arrogant and he didn't see the lifetime value of a customer.

Now, we have just said that I would go there 6 to 8 times a month; so, $600 to $800 a month. What could that be over 12 months? What could that be over 5 years? If you are treating one customer that way, and not seeing the lifetime value of that one customer, what are you losing? Well, we have just calculated here, let's be honest, that over a 12 month period, the significant amount of money, anywhere from $7,200 to $9,600 a year gone in one customer because of the owners attitude. He did not see the lifetime value of me.

My question to you is this: If he is doing that to me, how many other people is he doing it to? How many other people are not going back to that restaurant? Now, granted, they may not go with the same frequency that I was going, but they may decide to go less often or not even go at all after getting such bad service. Let's say that 10 customers decide not to return. Let's say that, on average, those 10 customers would have spent $2,000 a year in that one restaurant. That's $20,000 gone, wasted, because they have not seen the lifetime value of a customer. They have seen the initial sale that walked through the door for the very first time and said, "Let's try to get every penny we possible can out of them". Nothing frustrates me more than that. *(By the way my numbers are very conservative!)*

True wealth and stability within your business comes from repeat business. Repeat customers.

This one area can massively turn your business around. Just by now consciously becoming aware that you need to look after your customers with future interactions in mind. You want them to keep coming back, giving you more and more money, and in return for the money you are going to give them outstanding service, and an outstanding experience. In the long run, you want to give them a reason to want to come back. You don't want their money to go in someone else's pocket. That one is a no brainer.

Also, have a look and figure out what products you sell. Do you know that most companies are unaware of the volume of products or services they sell? List them. List your products or services and be aware of them. Then have a look to see what customers have bought what products and services. Then contact the customers with offers on the products or services that they haven't bought.

Here is a great statistic for you. The easiest thing to sell is an existing product to an existing customer. A more *difficult* thing to do is to sell a *new* product to an *existing* customer. Three times more difficult is selling a new customer an existing product, and four times more difficult, the hardest thing to do of all, is selling a new product to a new customer. That in itself tells us we need to focus on our *existing* customers.

A concept of mine I like to talk about is 'THE MATRIX OF AWESOME!' It is the easiest and most powerful tool to allow you to maximize your sales and profits of your entire product or service line to your existing customer base. This unlocks hidden profits within your business. If you want more information about 'THE MATRIX OF AWESOME!', you can either follow this url or use the QR code:

www.TheMatrixOfAwesome.com

This website will give you FREE information that can bring in massive profits to your business. You can even find there a downloadable Audio version from the book for FREE...! you're welcome!

I am all about making things easy. Things are difficult enough in life as it is, so why do we need to over-complicate things? We don't, and we shouldn't. So, make a list of all the other products or services that you could sell your customer. What are the things that you could sell, and then send them an offer: "We just got these new 'things'. You are a great customer of ours. We really appreciate you being our customer, and we really want to look after you. So much so, we have just come out with this new product; we actually believe the product or service will massively benefit you, and this is why we believe that... We know that, looking back at what you have bought in the past, you have bought this type of product or service, and this new item fits right in there, and it fits in there because of this". Educate, educate, educate. Educate the customer.

Now, they may not turn out and buy it. It doesn't matter. What matters is that you have gone to them and offered them something because you believe that it is truly beneficial to them, and you are not out there just trying to get their money.

This is quite a mind-blowing section; when you really take the time to analyze and think about it properly, how much more money you could bring in just by going the extra distance of looking after your customer. So, look really hard into this.

Take some time right now. If you have not already gone to the notes section, go to it now. What can you do right now to start thinking about the lifetime value of your customers? What are the things you could implement? What are the systems that

you need to start building?

Notes:

Do you consider the lifetime value of your customer?

How often do you want your customer to continue to come and buy from you? How many potential customers are you losing?

List your products and services that you currently sell. Are you selling all these to your existing customers?

What are the systems that you could put in place to build on your current and potential clientele?

Conclusion

So, let me wrap this up nicely: by looking after our customers and giving them a positive experience of doing business with us, they will want to continue to come back to us over and over again.

We need to start to understand what happens in our industry, understand what the norm is, look at the way we do things, figure out if we conform to our industry. If we do what our industry does, then we need to figure out how we can start to separate ourselves, and we can do that by adapting and adopting other ideas and things that we've noticed from different businesses in different industries. We're going to look to see what works, and what we think would work. We're going to implement it the 'JFDI' way. We're going to watch it carefully. We're going to see how the customer responds to that. If we get positive responses, we're going to make those new practices part of doing business with us every single time. We are going to systemize them.

If we receive negative responses from our customers, we're going to consciously be aware of it, and then remove it from our business. We're going to weed out the bad things in our business and we're going to increase the good things in our business, even if we've taken them from another business or another industry and adapted and adopted those aspects into our business.

We're going to look now and notice if our service has slipped over time, and if it has slipped, how can we improve on it. If it has not slipped, how can we improve it anyway? If we're not moving forward, we are moving backwards because other businesses are moving forward. Status quo is not an option, we get left behind if we don't take action.

You're going to notice now how many other businesses don't look after their customers. You're going to notice this every time you're now out. Use this to trigger your brain to start working consciously, not sub-consciously. Growth can only be made consciously.

When we work in a conscious state, when we know what works, then we can make that happen all the time. Remember the story about the two golfers.

Then you're going to notice which businesses are good and how they look after their customers. We're going to look at different things that we notice that we love, when we receive an experience of good service or just good ways of doing business. We're going to then adopt and adapt it to our business to make it relevant, and we're going to make sure that that happens every single time by every single member of our staff every time a customer comes to our business. We do that by putting a system in place.

We looked at examples of how businesses *used* to run, how businesses used to care about the customer. Think about what you can do now to show that you care, to show that you're going the extra mile.

We spoke about how, when we make decisions about our business, how we base those decisions around looking after the customer as a whole, not as an individual. And we start to build our business around giving outstanding service to our customer, the whole customer.

We briefly touched on how we noticed that most businesses really only care about themselves. They don't care about the customer. So, becoming consciously aware of that and actually caring about the customer, that in it-self will make us stand out from the rest.

We spoke about the huge importance that staff can have when it comes to service. Do we have the right staff? Are we employing for attitude and teaching skill? If we are a service-based business, it has to be all about the service, doesn't it?

If you are a personal fitness trainer and you're a 'one-man-band', it's about you giving the customer an experience every single time you are with them so they don't go find another personal trainer. Because, there are a lot out there, aren't there? As there is with any business or service or product.

We're going to keep in constant contact with the customer. We're going to let them know that sometimes we don't have even any information for them, but that we thought enough about them to call and let them know that we've not forgotten about them. We're going to keep in contact with the customer on a constant basis, even if there is no problem, even if they're not in a buying process. When we keep in contact with them, we're going to keep educating them about the product or service, who we are, what we do, and why we do the things we do. Why we are the business to come and deal with. Why we're different. How we're different. We can do that in many different ways. We can do it via a telephone call, via email, via online videos, by direct mail, by a handwritten note. There are multiple ways that we can now keep in contact with a customer and educate them. We all love to be educated on things we love or are interested in during that moment in time of our life.

We spoke about how, when things go wrong and a customer gets a bad experience, we can turn an OW into a WOW, and how we can blow them out of the water. In so doing, we can begin to create raving fans that sing our praises, that love us, that tell other people about us, and that want to keep coming back to us.

We spoke about how going the extra mile has such a positive impact on your business and how other businesses never do that. Maybe they don't know. Maybe they just don't care. I know that when we look back on our own personal experiences, we have all dealt with businesses that just don't care. So, begin to care. Begin to do something that is more than the way you currently do it; that is more than the current standards within your industry.

We spoke about quality control and the importance of making sure that, when you serve that food out of your 'Hell's Kitchen', that food is going out perfectly all the time. Even if you remove 'Gordon Ramsey' from 'The Pass', you make sure that the new person that stands at 'The Pass' have the same values and beliefs and standards that 'Gordon Ramsey' does. You want to make sure that quality control is exactly the same in every member of the staff, and all of it can be easily systemized.

What are your standards? Write them down. How do you go above and beyond? Write it down. Make all information clearly known to every member of your staff. Let them know what you expect of them and what will get them fired. Then, how are you going to get this information out to your staff? Do you have a staff handbook? Do you send it out via memo? I don't know. That's up to you. It depends on the size of your business.

That doesn't matter; what does matter is that it actually happens. **JFDI!**

We spoke about the lifetime value of a customer and how we do not want to be looking at the customer only as the initial sale.

I remember being a kid, I've always had a love for sports cars. To me, they are moving pieces of art. I remember, I had just passed my driving test. I was driving down the street and I came across a car dealership of a specific car I loved. So, I called in there this one time and they totally ignored me. "Look at this young kid here. He hasn't got enough money to be able to buy one of these cars". It was true, I didn't, at that time. I wasn't anywhere near it. But, a few years later, I was. And, a few years later, I went in and I bought that sports car, but you know what? I didn't buy it from that dealer. Why? Because they had no time for me then. And eight years later, I went elsewhere. Eight years! I still ended up buying the product. I ended up buying the car. I just found somebody else to buy it from because I remembered how they made me feel then and I didn't want to give them my money. Does that make sense?

We looked at the 80/20 rule, and we started to recognize who the top 20% of our customers are. We start to work on the 20%, buying all of our products or services.

So, the whole book has been about raising your conscious level of awareness in your business when it comes to service, when it comes to looking after your customers. It's also
134

about going above and beyond and giving them an experience every time they either do business with you or even have contact with you.

I want to thank you for taking the time to read this book. I truly hope that it has enlightened you in so many different areas, and one day I look forward to hearing your story when you come to me or contact me through email, or stand in front of me at one of my seminars. I want to see and hear how these changes have impacted your life and your business, because when your business starts to run effortlessly because you come from a place of giving, your life will also come from a place of love and giving. The line between personal life and business is very, very fine. Money is a by-product of a heart and mind that is harmonically balanced. It just comes naturally, because you now come from a different place internally.

www.ianhoughton.com

Additional space for notes:

Additional space for notes:

Additional space for notes:

Additional space for notes:

Additional space for notes: